Recent Themes in
Early American History

Historians in Conversation:
Recent Themes in Understanding the Past
Series editor, Louis A. Ferleger

Recent Themes in
EARLY AMERICAN HISTORY

Historians in Conversation

Edited by Donald A. Yerxa

The University of South Carolina Press

© 2008 University of South Carolina

Published by the University of South Carolina Press
Columbia, South Carolina 29208

www.sc.edu/uscpress

Manufactured in the United States of America

17 16 15 14 13 12 11 10 09 08   10 9 8 7 6 5 4 3 2 1

Library of Congress Cataloging-in-Publication Data

Recent themes in early American history : historians in conversation / edited by Donald A. Yerxa.
    p. cm. — (Historians in conversation)
    Includes bibliographical references and index.
    ISBN 978-1-57003-764-1 (cloth : alk. paper) — ISBN 978-1-57003-765-8 (pbk : alk. paper)
    1. United States—History—Colonial period, ca. 1600–1775—Historiography. 2. United States—History—Revolution, 1775–1783—Historiography. 3. United States—History—1783–1865—Historiography. I. Yerxa, Donald A., 1950–
    E187.2.R43 2008
    973.2—dc22
                                                                 2008020505

Contents

Series Editor's Preface *vii*
Acknowledgments *ix*

Introduction: Some Thoughts on the Present Robust and Disorderly State of Early American History *1*
Donald A. Yerxa

PART 1. THE STATE OF EARLY AMERICAN HISTORY: A FORUM

Disjunctions in Early American History *9*
Pauline Maier
The Promise of Empire *18*
Edward G. Gray
Continuity and Change in Early American Studies *24*
Don Higginbotham
Comments on Pauline Maier's "State of the Field" *28*
Peter S. Onuf
Political History's Demise? *33*
Paul A. Rahe
An Agenda for Early American History *37*
Jack N. Rakove
Rejoinder *41*
Pauline Maier

PART 2. THE COLONIAL PERIOD

Richard Hakluyt's Problem *47*
Peter C. Mancall
Jamestown Redivivus: An Interview with James Horn *53*
Conducted by Randall J. Stephens
Re-Bunking the Pilgrims *59*
Jeremy Dupertuis Bangs
What Happened to the Puritans? *67*
Thomas S. Kidd

The Great Meadow: Sustainable Husbandry in Colonial Concord   *73*
Brian Donahue

The Colonial Colleges: Forging an American Political Culture   *83*
J. David Hoeveler

Groping for National Identity by Forging a National Cuisine   *91*
James E. McWilliams

PART 3. REVOLUTION AND THE EARLY REPUBLIC

Local Authority and the Origins of the U.S. Constitution   *101*
Gordon S. Wood

An Interview with John Ferling   *109*
Conducted by Joseph S. Lucas

A World of Kings   *121*
Brendan McConville

1816: A Year of Transition   *128*
C. Edward Skeen

Further Readings   *135*
Contributors   *143*
Index   *147*

Series Editor's Preface

The Historical Society was founded in 1997 to create more venues for common conversations about the past. Consequently, in the autumn of 2001, the Historical Society launched a new type of publication. The society's president, George Huppert, and I believed that there was an important niche for a publication that would make the work of the most prominent historians more accessible to nonspecialists and general readers. We recruited two historians who shared this vision, Joseph S. Lucas and Donald A. Yerxa, and asked them to transform *Historically Speaking* into a journal of historical ideas. Up to that point, *Historically Speaking* had served as an in-house publication reporting on the society's activities and its members' professional accomplishments. Yerxa and Lucas quickly changed the layout and content of *Historically Speaking*, and within a short period of time many of the most prominent historians in the world began appearing in its pages—people such as Danielle Allen, Niall Ferguson, Daniel Walker Howe, Mary Lefkowitz, Pauline Maier, William McNeill, Geoffrey Parker, and Sanjay Subrahmanyam. *Historically Speaking*'s essays, forums, and interviews have drawn widespread attention. The *Chronicle of Higher Education*'s "Magazine and Journal Reader" section, for example, repeatedly has highlighted pieces appearing in *Historically Speaking*. And leading historians are loyal readers, praising *Historically Speaking* as a "must-read" journal, a "*New York Review of Books* for history," and "the most intellectually exciting publication in history that is currently available."

The Historical Society is pleased to partner with the University of South Carolina Press to publish a multivolume series, *Historians in Conversation: Recent Themes in Understanding the Past*. Each thematic volume pulls key essays, forums, and interviews from *Historically Speaking* and makes them accessible for classroom use and for the general reader. The original selections from *Historically Speaking* are supplemented with an introductory essay by Donald A. Yerxa along with suggestions for further reading.

We welcome your interest in the Historical Society. You may find us on the Internet at www.bu.edu/historic. You may also contact us at the Historical Society, 656 Beacon St., Mezzanine, Boston, Mass., 02215-2010, telephone 617-358-0260.

LOUIS A. FERLEGER

Acknowledgments

This volume contains a number of essays and interviews that appeared in the pages of *Historically Speaking* from 2004 to 2007. I am indebted to the gifted historians who have contributed to the publication over the past several years and especially those whose work appears in this volume. Brendan McConville, whose perceptive analysis of early American history I have relied upon liberally, in particular deserves acknowledgment. I have been blessed to work with terrific colleagues at *Historically Speaking* and the Historical Society. It is especially a joy to work with Joseph S. Lucas, my coeditor, and Randall Stephens, our associate editor. Both are superb historians, first-rate editors, and great friends. And my wife, Lois, has been a constant source of encouragement and support.

Introduction

Some Thoughts on the Present Robust and Disorderly State of Early American History

Donald A. Yerxa

In 1995 the distinguished historian Gordon S. Wood referred to the outpouring of scholarship on early America as "an embarrassment of riches." "Writing about the colonial period," he added, "has virtually exploded."[1] About the same time in another publication, Wood also commented on the discontinuity between the colonial and national periods of American history evident in the work of early American historians.[2] Looking at this field from an outsider's perspective—that of a generalist historian and editor—nothing that has transpired since the mid-1990s that would prompt me to challenge Wood's depiction of the state of early American historiography. The field is remarkably robust in terms of the diversity and sheer volume of work being published, but it has expanded in so many directions that one could argue that it is in some disarray. This is the contention of one of Wood's former students, Brendan McConville.[3] His assessment of the state of early American history is perceptive and well worth repeating here at the outset of a volume of essays on this period.

Undoubtedly, the most striking thing about the current state of early American history is the field's expansion in recent decades. Assisted by a variety of electronic tools—not the least of which is Readex's Archive of Americana—early American history, McConville notes, has expanded chronologically, geographically, and topically. He contends that early American historiography exhibits "chronological imperialism" as it has expanded forward into the nineteenth century to include the "Age of Jackson" and backward into the seventeen century. The field has also expanded geographically. Colonial America has lost its Anglocentric focus. It is no longer confined to the British colonies strung along the Atlantic seaboard but includes the entire continent in the seventeenth and eighteenth centuries.[4] Alan Taylor's volume in the Penguin History of the United States series, *American Colonies,* is perhaps the best example of the "continentalist" approach. Taylor notes that in traditional renderings of colonial history, the colonies of rival European empires were generally treated as "a hazy backdrop of hostility: backward threats to the English America that alone spawned the American Revolution and the United States." And the American West did not appear until invaded by the United States in the nineteenth century.[5] The study of those British seaboard colonies, moreover, has also been placed into the much-larger geographical context of the Atlantic world, a massive "zone of exchange and interchange, circulation, and transmission."[6]

Along with chronological and geographical expansions, the field of early American history has also greeted an abundance of new topics and approaches in recent decades. The subjects early American historians now investigate include "slavery, gender, gender relations, sexuality, ethnicity, Native Americans, sailors, pirates, and most recently music, signing, and food ways, have all become part of early American history."[7] This trend was well under way back in 1995 when Wood noted, "There is scarcely an aspect of human behavior in early America that historians today do not write about—from divorce to dying, from consumption of goods to child rearing."[8] According to Taylor, most of the changes in the field in recent decades "reflect the influence of cultural and linguistic studies." The use of ethnographic tools has helped historians recover the worlds of Native Americans, moving them from the periphery much closer to the center of many narratives. Gender has emerged as a major category of analysis, and to quote Taylor again, "Race is understood actively, daily constructed rather than as a universal given."[9]

McConville argues that the "shift to cultural studies–influenced history" has generated "a major intellectual fault line" in the field of early American history. Many historians have embraced cultural studies and write about such things as "discourse, the body, the public sphere, ritual, and print culture."[10] Others react to this cultural turn in the field with skepticism and even hostility. And, of course, there are those in the middle who accept the new scholarship provided it is based on solid evidence. McConville suspects that these divisions reflect generational, gender, and even political differences among early Americanists. But he is especially concerned that at the core of these divisions is a lack of consensus on research standards and the appropriate relationship between theory and archival research.[11] His own take is that early American historians have become too dependent on frameworks imported from social and linguistic theorists—people like Michel de Certeau, Michel Foucault, Stephen Greenblatt, Benedict Anderson, and Jürgen Habermas. What is needed, rather, is a reconceptualization of the field based on a careful reading of the bountiful archival and print materials.[12] The field's chronological frameworks also need to be rethought. Periodization schemes reveal historians' notions regarding the continuities and discontinuities of the past. And McConville encourages early Americanists, as they reconsider their chronological schemes, to pay attention to "how people of the period thought of time, history, and change."[13]

The expansiveness of early American historiography, measured both qualitatively and quantitatively, clearly indicates a very robust field. But McConville rightly worries that early American history is also a field in "considerable disarray." For example, the geographical expansion of early American history has "decentered the field's traditional narrative in which histories of the thirteen colonies come to be united through the Revolution."[14] He admits that the old narrative was too whiggish, but at least it provided coherence.[15] Taylor, whose work illustrates well both the geographical and topical expansiveness of the field, acknowledges that writing colonial history "used to be easier, because the human cast and geographic stage were both considered so much smaller." But the coherence of older narratives came at far too high a price: "Until the 1960s, most American historians," Taylor contends, "assumed that 'the colonists' meant English-speaking men confined to the Atlantic seaboard. Women were there as passive and inconsequential helpmates. Indians were wild and primitive peoples beyond the pale: unchanging objects of colonists' fears and aggressions. African slaves appeared as unfortunate aberrations in a fundamentally upbeat story of Englishmen becoming freer and more prosperous by colonizing an open land."[16] Of course, McConville is not arguing that historians retain an inadequate and outdated narrative of early America just because it offers coherence. And it may well be that a single dominant narrative theme or central focus will not emerge. But the expansion of the field challenges historians to devise new themes that provide a greater measure of coherence than we now have.[17]

Disorderly expansiveness is certainly not unique to early American historiography. There has been a similar "embarrassment of riches" in many other historical fields. As is the case for early American history, the avalanche of recent historical scholarship has yielded a richly complex past. Many, if not most, traditional historiographical frameworks are being challenged, and there is little consensus as to what will replace them. This is to be expected. Robust fields are not known for being tidy, and a certain amount of conceptual and historiographical messiness will always accompany intellectual ferment. Regrettably, however, in some fields—the history of early modern science comes to mind[18]—historians who have embraced the novelty and complexity of the new scholarship have also questioned whether an underlying coherence to their fields is possible or even desirable. Taylor's comments about colonial history a half century ago demonstrate that frameworks offering coherence can portray a false past reality stripped of complexity. That said, the cost of incoherence is far too steep. As I have argued elsewhere, absent the search for coherence, historical inquiry flirts with intellectual bankruptcy, and historians risk becoming guardians of antiquarianism. Because historians have an important social responsibility to make sense of the past,[19] a more constructive response to recent historical scholarship is to refine and, where needed, replace existing frameworks with new ones that offer a more coherent rendering of a more complex past. New findings should —and generally do—prompt the search for more intricate patterns and frameworks.[20] Anything less should be lamented and resisted.

No single volume can adequately reflect all the currents of early American historiography. This volume of essays and interviews appearing in the pages of *Historically Speaking* from 2004 to 2007 certainly makes no claim to do so. It has more-modest goals: to demonstrate that traditional approaches still powerfully illuminate our understanding of the early American past and that good scholars continue to make fresh contributions to traditional topics.

The centerpiece of the book is a forum based on Pauline Maier's essay on the disjunctions of early American history. She enters the long-standing debate in American historiography about the relationship of colonial to national history[21] and argues that the disjunction between colonial and Revolutionary historiography is the result of "new understandings as well as historians' creative re-definitions of colonial America." She is careful to add that she does not criticize this disjunction but notes it. A cast of distinguished historians—Edward G. Gray, Don Higginbotham, Peter S. Onuf, Paul A. Rahe, and Jack Rakove—respond, followed by a brief rejoinder from Maier.

In separate essays, Wood and McConville also speak to this question. Wood reveals one significant way in which the colonial and early national eras were linked. He makes the case for continuity between the localization of political authority in the colonial era and the ideas of federalism and separation of powers that the framers incorporated in 1787. McConville rejects teleological notions that view the colonial period as "a long prologue to the revolutionary crisis or American society's broader modernization" and argues that colonial political culture from 1689 to 1775 was profoundly royalist in ways historians often ignore.

Maier also briefly discusses another disjunction, that between "scholarly interests and those of the reading public." Nowhere is this more apparent than in reaction to the outpouring of studies about the Founding generation. The public appetite for these books is enormous. But some historians dismiss work focusing so heavily on white male elites.[22] John Ferling, a distinguished practitioner of traditional political and military history and author of several best-selling books on the founders, comments on his work and career. C. Edward Skeen, another traditionalist, implicitly rejects the notions of Benedict Anderson and his followers that the nation is invented or imagined. He explores a standard theme in traditional American political history, the emergence of American nationalism, by looking at a single year, 1816.

Several authors in this volume reexamine standard topics in fresh ways. Peter C. Mancall emphasizes Richard Hakluyt's important role in advancing English colonization. James Horn talks about the importance and legacy of Jamestown and contends it has been overshadowed by all the attention paid to the Plymouth colony. Jeremy Dupertuis Bangs, however, reacts strongly to ways in which the Pilgrims and Plymouth colony are portrayed in textbooks today. Thomas S. Kidd reevaluates the end of Puritanism and makes the case that after 1689 many New Englanders became attached to the "'Protestant interest,' the faithful community of world Protestants fighting against world Catholicism." Early American historians, Kidd argues, should view this Protestant interest as the link between Puritanism and evangelicalism. J. David Hoeveler looks at the history of colonial colleges and examines their contributions to the emerging political culture in early America.

A few essays in this volume illustrate the topical expansiveness of recent early American historiography. Brian Donahue's essay on husbandry and land use in colonial Concord, Massachusetts, provides a fascinating and insightful look at landscape and the environment in colonial farming, one that challenges the view that colonial farmers were wasteful of resources, clearing new land rather than caring intensively for what they already had in cultivation. James E. McWilliams looks at how cooking and eating in the early nineteenth century helped Americans forge a national identity and figure out who they were.

NOTES

1. Gordon S. Wood, "A Century of Writing Early American History: Then and Now Compared; or How Henry Adams Got It Wrong," *American Historical Review* 100, no. 3 (June 1995): 687.

2. Gordon S. Wood, "The Relevance and Irrelevance of American Colonial History," in *Imagined Histories: American Historians Interpret the Past*, ed. Anthony

Molho and Gordon S. Wood (Princeton: Princeton University Press, 1998), 157–60. Wood's essay was drawn from a paper he gave at a conference held in 1995, so the commentary is essentially simultaneous with that of his *AHR* essay cited in note 1.

3. Brendan McConville, "Early America in a New Century: Decline, Disorder, and the State of Early American History," *Journal of the Historical Society* 5, no. 4 (2005): 461–82.

4. Ibid., 470–72.

5. Alan Taylor, *American Colonies* (New York: Viking, 2001), x.

6. McConville, "Early America in a New Century," 471. The description of the Atlantic world is from Trevor Burnard, "Only Connect: The Rise and Rise (and Fall) of Atlantic History," *Historically Speaking* 7, no. 6 (July/August 2006): 20.

7. McConville, "Early America in a New Century," 471.

8. Wood, "A Century of Writing Early American History," 688.

9. Alan Taylor, "Interchange: The Practice of History," *Journal of American History* 90, no. 2 (September 2003): 577–78. See Joyce E. Chaplin's assessment of the impact of ethnohistory on early American historiography in "Expansion and Exceptionalism in Early American History," *Journal of American History* 89, no. 4 (March 2003): 1447–49.

10. The list is from Chaplin, "Expansion and Exceptionalism," 1446.

11. McConville, "Early America in a New Century," 471–72.

12. Ibid., 474–75.

13. Ibid., 475–76.

14. Ibid., 469–71.

15. Ibid.

16. Taylor, *American Colonies*, x.

17. McConville, "Early America in a New Century," 470–71.

18. See H. Floris Cohen, "Reconceptualizing the Scientific Revolution," *European Review* 15, no. 4 (October 2007): 491–502. For a superb analytical discussion of the notion of coherence in historical study, see Allan Megill, "Coherence and Incoherence in Historical Studies: From the Annales School to the New Cultural History," *New Literary History* 35 (2004): 207–31.

19. Donald A. Yerxa, "Historical Coherence, Complexity, and the Scientific Revolution," *European Review* 15, no. 4 (October 2007): 439–44.

20. John Hedley Brooke, "Science, Religion, and Historical Complexity," *Historically Speaking* 8, no. 5 (May/June 2007): 12.

21. See Wood, "Relevance and Irrelevance," 157–60, and Jack P. Greene, "Colonial History and National History: Reflections on a Continuing Problem," *William and Mary Quarterly* 64, no. 2 (April 2007): 235–50.

22. See Alan Taylor, review of *Beyond the Founders: New Approaches to the Political History of the Early Republic*, ed. Jeffrey L. Palsey, Andrew W. Robertson, and David Waldstreicher, *William and Mary Quarterly* 62, no. 4 (October 2005): 764–67. For a different interpretation of the recent literature on the founders, one that sees it as a vibrant discourse, see Trevor Burnard, "The Founding Fathers in Early American Historiography: A View from Abroad," *William and Mary Quarterly* 62, no. 4 (October 2005): 745–64.

PART 1

The State of Early American History

A Forum

Disjunctions in Early American History

Pauline Maier

My assignment is to assess "the state of the field" in colonial and Revolutionary history. I am not going to do that book by book, topic by topic. That would be tedious, and I assume you know the basic story. In the past few decades, historical research has shifted, by and large, from political to social and then cultural history. Some of the most dramatic additions to historical knowledge have come in the history of slavery, including the slave trade and African American history; in women's history; and in the study of Native Americans.

What I want to do in the brief time I have is to step back and call attention to three significant "disjunctions" that characterize the intellectual landscape with reference to early American history and, to some extent, American history in general.

The first is between colonial and Revolutionary history, the two periods that are our focus today. In preparation for this occasion, I attended "state of the field" sessions on the colonial and Revolutionary periods at the Organization of American Historians (OAH) meeting in Boston last March. In the second session, someone commented that the two fields seem entirely unconnected. The truth is that's been the case for a long time.

When I began teaching in the late 1960s, my course on colonial America —really colonial British America—focused in good part on the "new social history," particularly the demographic studies of communities first in New England, then the Chesapeake. In 1972 Alfred Crosby's *Columbian Exchange: Biological and Cultural Consequences of 1492* appeared, awakening

Professor Maier's essay is adapted from a lecture she gave at a National Endowment for the Humanities forum on April 30, 2004. It originally appeared in the July/August 2004 issue of *Humanities*. A slightly edited version was published in *Historically Speaking* 6 (March/April 2005) with the permission of the NEH. The several responses and Maier's rejoinder were specifically commissioned for *Historically Speaking*.

widespread consciousness of the demographic catastrophe among Native Americans that followed their first encounters with Europeans and the possible connections between New World foods and population growth in other parts of the world. Already some fine studies were available on the origins of American slavery; others studied that institution from a cross-cultural perspective. To be sure, I also discussed topics such as religion and the structure of politics and political institutions in British North America.

Even so, after the term break, when I taught the American Revolution, the traditional successor course to colonial America, the difference was like night and day. The old Progressive interpretation of the Revolution, which stressed social conflict and elite manipulation of the masses, lay in tatters. Scholars were taking the ideas of the Revolution seriously, tracing their origins, and revealing their impact on the evolution of political institutions. To be sure, any course on the Revolution has to include a discussion of pre-American society and of the Revolution's social impact. I cannot, for example, imagine teaching the Revolution without citing Jack P. Greene's *Pursuits of Happiness: The Social Development of Early Modern British Colonies and the Formation of American Culture* (1988), particularly his emphasis on the "extraordinarily large number of families of independent middling status" in the British North American colonies: they were, he wrote, "proportionately substantially more numerous than in any other contemporary Western society." (And every time I read that sentence aloud, I wonder whether Jack really needed those two contiguous adverbs.) Still, by and large, the study of colonial America was social; the study of the Revolution political and ideological.

Three-plus decades later, colonial American history remains strikingly different from the study of the American Revolution but for different reasons. Historians of early America are now more than ever anxious to avoid earlier emphases on the British settlers of North America, the teleology implicit in studying only those colonies that would later become the United States, and what Harvard's Joyce Chaplin referred to in the March 2003 *Journal of American History* as "that persistent myth, American exceptionalism." The most prominent public participants in the American Revolution were white men of European descent who founded the American republic believing that accomplishment marked a break from the patterns of European history and so was by nature "exceptionalist." It's no surprise, then, that, as Chaplin notes, many particularly noteworthy examples of recent postcolonial scholarship focus on the early national rather than the Revolutionary period. David Waldstreicher's study of public celebrations, Joanne Freeman's book on honor in the politics of the 1790s, and Jill Lepore's *A Is for American* are examples.

What is "colonial history" today? There's no one answer. Alan Taylor's *American Colonies* (2001) suggests one conception of the field. The book discusses the Spanish, French, Dutch, and Swedish North American colonies along with those of Britain and the Russian colonization of Alaska. Taylor also devotes considerable space to Native American societies that do not qualify as colonies but were deeply affected by the arrival of Europeans and—for the Plains Indians in particular—the Spanish repatriation of the horse to its North American homeland. Taylor's book does not end, like traditional colonial history, in 1763 or 1776 but extends into the nineteenth century, when an "imperial" United States took over the Hispanic West. Clearly the book does not avoid the sin of teleology: the only reason to study Alaska is that it would eventually become part of the United States. But then the book was written as part of the Penguin History of the United States series.

The American Revolution does not have a prominent place in Taylor's book. Consider the opening sentences of its final paragraph: "The dominant colonial power on the Pacific rim became the United States, the hypercommercial nation founded by the Americans who won their independence from the British by revolution and war in the years 1775–83. Far from ending with the American Revolution, colonialism persisted in North America, but from a new base on the Atlantic seaboard."

I spend half a term on events to which he gives half a sentence. To be fair, earlier in the book, Taylor devotes another page and a quarter to the Revolution, a fraction of what he devotes to the Plains Indians. There he notes that the Americans' "empire of liberty" was for whites only and demanded the "systematic dispossession of native peoples and, until the Civil war . . . the perpetuation of black slavery." The "new American empire" also "provided military assistance to subdue Indians and Hispanics across the continent to the Pacific." In short, here the Revolution marks a moment in which a onetime colony became a colonizer. That has little to do with the Revolution as "the founding." It's simply a different story, one with little relevance for the one I teach, which focuses on the Revolutionary origins of American government.

Scholars who work under the banner of "Atlantic history" provide a rather different idea of how to study early American history, one that goes beyond North America to study "the common, comparative, and interactive aspects of the history of the peoples of the Atlantic world," as Bernard Bailyn explained in *The British Atlantic World, 1500–1800* (2002; edited by David Armitage and Michael J. Braddick). In theory, it involves all four continents that border the Atlantic and traditionally begins in 1492 and extends through the revolutions of the late eighteenth and nineteenth centuries, although some scholars are examining later periods from an "Atlantic perspective." Classic topics include "the movement of people, ideas of empire, cultural encounters, the circulation of ideas," and the Atlantic slave trade. That broad perspective appeals to members of "the current generation of historians," according to David Armitage, because it avoids the "constraints" of national history, particularly of a national history dominated by a concern with politics and constitutional development. Of course, the appeal is strong for historians of British North America in the period before the Revolution, when the "constraints" of national history are ahistorical and distort the perspectives and affiliations of the people they study.

Atlantic historians have the grace to admit that what they're doing is not entirely new: historians have been doing some form of Atlantic history since the late nineteenth century, and it became notably popular after World War II. Atlantic history often looks strangely familiar because so much work to date has focused on the British Atlantic World and most often the British World of the North Atlantic. In some ways, earlier generations stretched further: comparisons of the Spanish and British forms of colonial rule and slave systems were already de rigueur when I entered the field thirty-some years ago.

Atlantic history is not intrinsically hostile to political history or even to certain forms of national history so long as it's studied within an Atlantic context. The most novel work in recent years has, however, been outside the political—on trade, migrations both voluntary and coerced, the relationship of colonizers to indigenous peoples, and social structures, with particular reference to class, race, and gender. We know much more, for example, about slavery and the slave trade due to the Atlantic history of the past generation. How—and if—Atlantic history will affect the history of the American Revolution remains to be seen.

That's not to say new work has been without its influence on telling the story of the American Revolution. Historians now give more attention to the war in the west and the impact of the American victory on Indians than was once the case. And Ira Berlin's *Many Thousands Gone* (1998), a history of the first two centuries of slavery in North America that was written with an Atlantic perspective, provides a less upbeat version of the Revolution's impact on black Americans than, say, Arthur Zilversmit's *First Emancipation* (1967). But in general, as the study of colonial America has become both broader and less political, it has become different in content than the history of the Revolution.

Have the two fields ever been linked? Yes, back when Louis Hartz and others thought the real revolution came when Europeans first set foot on American soil, and the events of the 1760s and 1770s simply ratified that earlier historical reality. We don't believe that any more. British settlers, it seems, wanted nothing more than to approximate the model of British life, and as time went on, they did so to an increasing extent and so actually became more British by the eve of the Revolution than in the first settlements. That makes independence a break with the past that requires explanation, and I have spent a good part of my scholarly career wrestling with that issue. The point here, however, is that the disjunction of colonial and Revolutionary history is a result of new understandings as well as historians' creative redefinitions of colonial America. I don't criticize that disjunction. I simply note it.

My second disjunction can be described more quickly. It lies between scholarly interests and those of the reading public. In recent years, several books on the American founding have become best sellers. The most conspicuous examples are David McCullough's *John Adams* and Joseph Ellis's *Founding Brothers,* but many other books have also attracted a remarkably wide readership. According to an article by Jeffrey Trachtenberg in the April 12, 2004, *Wall Street Journal,* there are 550,000 hardback copies in print of Walter Isaacson's *Benjamin Franklin* and 75,000 hardback copies of David Fischer's *Washington's Crossing,* a history of the military campaign of 1776 and early 1777 that came out just a few months ago. That doesn't compare to the 1.6 million hardback copies of McCulloch's *Adams,* but in a day when few academic books sell 5,000 copies, it's impressive.

There are in fact more titles on the Revolution and the founding fathers published in the past few years than I have time to list, and more are on the way—a book on George Washington by Ellis due out in October, another on 1776 by McCullough that's supposed to appear next year. The appetite of the reading public seems almost insatiable. Most of the authors, however, are professional writers or historians of roughly my generation or, as with Edmund S. Morgan, the success of whose book on Franklin no doubt took Yale University Press by surprise, a generation older.

Younger historians, by and large, have abandoned the subject. Curiously they've done that just as the period became easier to study thanks to modern editions of the papers of Washington, Adams, Jefferson, Franklin, Hamilton, and Madison, as well as the multivolume *Documentary History of the Ratification of the Constitution* being published out of the State Historical Society of Wisconsin. Those published volumes make available to readers more documents than any scholar of an earlier generation was likely to read. They are, moreover, arranged chronologically, with letters to as well as from the person whose papers are published, are printed (the difference between print and handwritten manuscripts is major), and have introductions to provide context, footnotes to identify obscure references, and, joy of joys, *indices*. More documents generally mean new understandings, and more documents easier to use gilds the lily.

Obviously, professional writers are using these papers, richly repaying the public for those tax dollars the NEH used in subsidizing their publication. So are political scientists and historians in law schools: indeed, I more often find more younger scholars who are interested in what I do in political science departments and law schools than in history departments.

Why aren't young historians joining the party? Their disinterest is, again, part of a general movement against political history and the history of white men. And perhaps they assume incorrectly (as I did before doing research on the Declaration of Independence) that there's nothing new to learn: a young historian began a book review in last January's *William and Mary Quarterly* by commenting that "the literature on the founding period is . . . approaching saturation." Do they think, as Jack Rakove suggested to me recently, that all the big questions have been answered? Or simply that they have to write their dissertations on more "cutting edge" topics if they hope to get a job in this competitive market?

Whatever the reason, the effect is the same. As one audience member noted at the OAH state-of-the-field session, when he teaches the American Revolution, he finds himself assigning books that were published thirty years ago. (That's not all bad. I wrote one of those thirty-year-old books, which I hope he's assigning.)

Disjunction three is between historical scholarship and history as taught in secondary school or, more exactly, history as taught in secondary schools and history as taught in college-level U.S.-survey courses. Whether it's in fashion or not, schoolteachers have to cover political history: it's part of the basic knowledge students in the United States need, if only as part of their civic education. More surprising, a set of interviews by Gary Kornblith and Carol Laser of Oberlin College—which were published in the 2001 *Journal of American History*—discovered that teachers of the U.S. survey (i.e., the basic college course on American history) feel the same obligation. That discovery was all the more striking because Kornblith and Laser took the trouble to recruit survey teachers from different generations and with correspondingly different assumptions and scholarly proclivities. Nonetheless, they all seemed to understand the reaction of a young historian who, almost to his surprise, was appalled by a student who had no idea what Reconstruction was.

Of course, neither the best secondary schoolteachers nor teachers of the U.S. survey want to teach the same thing over and over; they need to integrate new learning into their courses. Sometimes that's easy, as, for example, with demographic history or black history, which extend and enrich the traditional, basically political narrative. Sometimes it's challenging. And sometimes it's impossible. Hostility toward national histories is fine and good —unless you happen to be down for teaching the first half of the U.S. survey in the fall or are preparing students for the college-board examinations. Redefine the subject, you might say; teach global history instead. Why "instead"? And there's a cost to taking that route: more college graduates with no idea what Reconstruction is or how the Constitution was written and why. If some historians are prepared to live with that type of historical illiteracy, other Americans are not. Traditional history, as the NEH "We the People" initiative demonstrates, has powerful advocates.

The ultimate historical question is always, "So what?" What difference does it make that colonial and Revolutionary history have gone their separate ways, that popular historians (along with political scientists, legal historians, and some senior historians) have picked up the story of the founding as young historians choose to study other topics, that secondary teachers and college professors teaching the U.S. survey have to cover topics no longer at the front of historians' scholarly agenda? Not much, you might say.

How enduring are these disjunctions likely to be? I'm a historian, not a prophet—a distinction I often find useful. But in hazarding a guess, we have the advantage of Ellen Fitzpatrick's *History's Memory: Writing America's Past, 1880–1980* (2002), a gem of a book that never got the attention it deserved. Fitzpatrick demonstrates—with a wit and a moral consciousness rare in historiography—that social and cultural history, including the history of minorities and women, and even terms like "the new history" have been endemic in American historical writing since the late nineteenth century. Always these "new" initiatives were poised against political history, and yet it survived. The problem is that historians tend to forget their predecessors—thus the irony in her title. In that regard the Atlantic historians seem truly exceptional in acknowledging and building upon the work of earlier generations.

Scholarship between the 1960s and 1980s on the Revolution was so intense that the subject was perhaps destined to go into a certain eclipse. Once the old answers to big questions lose their persuasiveness or new ways of approaching familiar material come into view, there's no doubt it will become a more active field. There's already evidence that's happening—and, indeed, that political history as a whole is reviving. Take, for example, a book of essays edited by my colleague Margaret Jacobs with William Novak and Julian Zelizer, entitled *The Democratic Experiment: New Directions in American Political History* (2003). A session devoted to that book at the recent OAH meeting attracted so large a crowd, I'm told, that both the room and the hall outside were packed. Latecomers couldn't even get near the door.

Let me give another example that concerns the Revolution. Max Edling's *Revolution in Favor of Government: Origins of the U.S. Constitution and the Making of the American State* (2003) is a small book—with about 230 pages of basic text—that makes a big argument. Briefly stated, it denies that nationalists advocated a major revision of the country's central government in the late 1780s in order to check a persistent misuse of power by democratic state legislatures. That interpretation, which has, by and large, dominated the field since Gordon S. Wood's *Creation of the American Republic* appeared in the late 1960s, is founded to a considerable extent on James Madison's preconvention memo "The Vices of the System." Wood even entitled the relevant part of his book "Vices of the System." But Edling says that Madison was not a characteristic nationalist. Most advocates of the Constitution wanted to form a "fiscal-military state" like those of contemporary Europe. As a result, the creation and ratification of the Constitution should be understood as an event in early modern "state formation."

Edling brings into question the reigning answer to an old question, gently attacks historians' recent fixation with Madison, and takes a major step toward understanding the American Revolution in an Atlantic context. I think that's promising. Surely Edling's book will affect the way I teach the U.S. survey next fall. Is it significant that Edling is a Swede who did his work at the University of Cambridge in England and Uppsala in Sweden? Young scholars in other countries are obviously more interested in the founding years of the American republic than are those in the United States.

There are other possible new approaches to the Revolution and new ways to make links with other fields and their insights. Economic historians, for example, are now deeply interested in the role of institutions as a determinant of economic development. Douglass C. North's *Institutions, Institutional Change, and Economic Performance* (1990) inspired much of that interest. The literature on that topic is comparative, characteristically looking at Latin America and the Caribbean against the United States and Canada. I cannot pretend to have read deeply in that literature, but what I've read suggests that where it refers to the American record for the late eighteenth and early nineteenth centuries, its empirical foundations are sometimes a tad weak. The opportunities for historians seem obvious. Surely young historians will soon realize, if they haven't already, that once-fashionable references to "imagined communities" and the "public sphere" have gone stale, and the time has come for a new departure.

So what am I doing? I'm writing a book on the ratification of the federal Constitution. That sounds like an old-fashioned topic, but there is no book in English devoted to telling the dramatic story of ratification. I've been using the modern *Papers of George Washington* for the Confederation Period and the *Documentary History of the Ratification of the Constitution*. And I've been finding a lot of evidence that runs against "established truths."

Thank God for age, or, if you prefer, seniority, and also tenure. They have given me freedom to follow my instincts, which is, I think, how the best historical work is done.

The Promise of Empire

Edward G. Gray

I would like to focus on the first of the three disjunctions Pauline Maier describes in her provocative essay: that between colonial and Revolutionary historiographies. She is entirely correct, it seems to me, in noting that disjunction. She is also right in suggesting that the disjunction is much more than a chronological or narrowly thematic one: it rests on a long-standing methodological divide between social historians and historians of the institutions of government. The former are engaged by the *longue durée* of the colonial era; the latter, by the *histoire evenementielle* of the comparatively brief Revolutionary era.

My own sense, though, is that far from growing more pronounced, this disjunction seems to be weakening. That's the good news. The bad news, from Maier's perspective, is that that weakening does not involve a return to the history of government. That is, to my knowledge, most young historians continue to avoid questions about the origins of the Constitution or the political thought of the founders or the power of the Continental Congress. Similarly there has been very little recent work on the apparatus of colonial government—whether the New England towns or the colonial assemblies. Exactly why historians have lost interest in the history of governing institutions is obviously connected to contemporary debates about exactly what it is we mean by politics. And among academic historians, the answer has hedged toward a capacious definition in which politics happens in the bedroom, in the coffeehouse, on the street, on ships at sea, and at the geographical fringes of European dominion. This trend has seemed to me driven less by any coherent agenda than by momentum (scholars have never gotten jobs by ignoring academic fashions) and an appetite for novelty. Of course, one historian's appetite for the new is another's exhaustion with the old. My sense is that the current fascination with narrative—much of which falls under the rubric microhistory or, as Robert Darnton recently dubbed one subgenre, "incident analysis"—comes not so much from some conscious postmodern nihilism as it does from a general exhaustion with overargued academic writing.[1]

Although we may lament the trend-driven habits of the academy, it seems to me some recent developments have much to offer those of us who have been frustrated by the disjunction between work in the colonial and Revolutionary periods. Put differently, these developments promise to alter the historical landscape so that questions about the creation of the United States can no longer be divorced from important questions about the colonies.

At the center of these developments has been the resurrection of empire as an explanatory device. The idea that events in the colonial and Revolutionary periods need to be understood in terms of the larger structures of the British Empire is not at all new; nor is there anything new about the idea that something called "empire" has long-term relevance in American history. What is relatively new is the notion that empire and all that it implied in the eighteenth century—the imperial bureaucracy, commercial networks, a distinct form of subjecthood, hierarchical legal and political regimes, and the like—allows us to view the whole disjointed eighteenth-century American past as a single, unified field of historical investigation.

It should be said that *empire*, as opposed to *the* or *an* empire, signifies, in addition to a kind of institution, a set of ideas and inclinations. It is akin to an *ism*, such as imperialism, although it carries far fewer negative connotations. The usage seems to be British in origin and parallels our own *democracy*. For Americans the latter is much more than a political order. It is a social disposition, an aesthetic, a philosophy, a collective identity, a form of material well-being, and so on. One need not trundle out Rudyard Kipling or that onetime Briton Benjamin Franklin (who wrote in an English newspaper in 1759 that New Englanders could scarcely be more British, given "their constant intercourse with *England,* by ships arriving almost every week from the capitol, their respect for the mother country, and admiration of every thing that is *British*"[2]) to see that *empire* has carried similar freight for the British. It has been much more than a system of colonial governance. It has also been—and perhaps still is—an economic agent, a frame of mind, a nationalist myth, an aesthetic field, and a kind of social currency. And if you look, you will find it everywhere—in literature, in painting, in architecture, in travel narratives, in diplomatic ritual, not to mention the minds and attitudes of statesmen and ordinary people.

Of the work that has assimilated this explanatory device, we might identify two categories. The first, animated in part by a desire to incorporate native peoples into the early American narrative, tends to focus on so-called backcountry or peripheral regions of the British Empire.[3] The second has illuminated the intellectual contours of eighteenth-century Anglo-American empire.[4] In terms of methodology, this work has very little in common. The former tends to draw more from social history and ethnohistory; the latter from intellectual and legal history. Similarly the core questions animating these two bodies of scholarship are different. The one asks how it was that the various constituents of a backcountry polity did or did not achieve a just political settlement. The other asks how statesmen and founders interpreted and rationalized the political geography of a Greater Britain. Despite these differences, there are important common concerns. The most obvious of these is the desire to understand early America in terms of some larger geographical frame, whether the Atlantic World or the continent of North America. A perhaps less-obvious, shared trait is the willingness to abandon crude assumptions about the Revolution's impact on the function and conception of empire in America.

Consider the following: historians have tended to associate early modern empire with a geography of power in which there is a clear center and periphery—the latter representing a steady dissipation of the controls exerted by the former. For students of the Revolution, this scheme helps set off the colonial period from what follows by presenting an easy contrast with the republic—at least as envisioned by Jefferson and his allies. For them, power is diffuse and localized, emanating from those very peripheries that empires render subordinate. What the backcountry work has shown, however, is that the periphery-center model is not really all that helpful for understanding actual backcountry politics before 1776. Rather than simply a broad dissipation of imperial authority, these areas experienced something more like blitzkrieg politics. During periods of diplomatic and military crisis, Britain, France, and their colonials worked (usually in futility) to establish authority and control. But during moments of imperial equilibrium, that project generally gave way to neglect. Similarly the status of subalterns changed very little with the Revolution. As Gregory Evans Dowd has recently noted, the old chestnut that Britain treated all peoples within the empire—whatever their skin color—as subjects while the United States denied nonwhites citizenship grossly oversimplifies the Revolutionary transition. In fact, under British rule (such as it was), Indians existed in a legal no-man's-land not all that different from their nonstatus in the United States. They were not quite subjects and not quite foreigners. As far as imperial politicians were concerned, the Indians' status was more like medieval subjects—children or dependents of the sovereign—than eighteenth-century subjects, the latter being less dependents than coinhabitants of the body politic.

What all this means is that in some regions, empire and everything it implied changed only nominally during the years of the Revolution. Blitzkrieg politics continued, violence remained the chief form of dispute resolution, and the status of native peoples (and to a lesser extent white Catholics) changed very little. The persistence of this backcountry political order raises important questions for Revolutionary historiography. Chief among these is to what extent did the founders think they would be able to do what the British never did? To what extent did they think they would be able to fashion a stable political order for the expanding American West? More to the point, to what extent did the founders' imperial vision differ from that of their British predecessors? As it turns out, according to the second body of scholarship I mention above, it differed less than we once thought.

Peter Onuf, for instance, has shown that Jefferson's own imperial vision owed much to a long-standing Anglo-American debate about the meaning and purpose of empire. At the center of that debate was the question of exactly how political order and empire were related. For Jefferson, the answer was, of course, some form of liberty. It was liberty that allowed the natural human affections to flourish, and it was liberty that would produce a natural and, for Jefferson, a healthy polity. At first glance, this appears to have very little to do with the British Empire. And indeed there is little in Jefferson's vision of what can be found in British imperial theorists, such as Thomas Pownall, for whom empire was something analogous to the modern idea of the state. But Pownall's vision was by no means universal. As J. G. A. Pocock has shown, for many British commentators, the idea of empire implied little more than nominal British sovereignty. It carried with it no firm imperatives about legal regimes or local modes of government. In effect, this empire looked a lot more like the diffuse, halo-like thing Jefferson envisioned than the rigid legal structures and commercial sinews the founders attacked during the imperial crisis.[5]

What this suggests is that the colonists' attack on the British Empire was actually quite British. It drew on a long-standing Anglo-American critique of empire, and it depended—at least as it would come to be articulated by Jefferson—on a remarkably British conception of empire. Could it thus be the case that to a degree we have yet to fully appreciate, Jack Greene was right some years ago when he wrote that "in contriving the Constitution, the framers had clearly drawn, if in many cases half-consciously, upon the experience and precedent of the empire?"[6]

Greene's insight raises a host of important questions. In what ways (if at all), for example, did the founders adjust British imperial theory—formulated above all for an oceanic empire—to serve the needs of a continental empire? Similarly, while we have Onuf's compelling work on Jefferson's notion of empire, our understanding of the Federalist vision remains superficial. We know little about the degree to which the Hamiltonian fiscal-military ideal did or did not draw on older British debates about the meaning of empire, particularly the legal regimes through which the British justified their various imperial projects. Finally the simple matter of exactly what empire came to mean to Americans after independence has not been systematically explored. Presumably, given Jefferson's formulation, the Revolution did not leave the idea with entirely negative connotations. Exactly why was this so? Did Americans distinguish between good and bad empire?[7]

As scholars assimilate the work I've described here, we can hope they begin to address these questions. We can also hope that they follow the lead of this work and recognize that, once again, the broader imperial context of the Revolution has much to teach us. But it will do so only if we abandon the whiggish tendency to divorce the behavior of the founders from that of the colonials they once were.

NOTES

1. Robert Darnton, "It Happened One Night," *New York Review of Books* 51, no. 11 (June 24, 2004): 60–64.

2. Benjamin Franklin quoted in J. A. Leo Lemay, ed., *Benjamin Franklin: Writings* (New York: Library of America, 1987), 520.

3. An incomplete list of this work includes Fred Anderson, *Crucible of War: The Seven Years' War and the Fate of Empire in British North America, 1754–1766* (New York: Knopf, 2000); Gregory Evans Dowd, *War under Heaven: Pontiac, the Indian Nations, & the British Empire* (Baltimore: Johns Hopkins University Press, 2002); Eric Hinderaker, *Elusive Empires: Constructing Colonialism in the Ohio Valley, 1673–1800* (Cambridge, U.K.: Cambridge University Press, 1997); Jane T. Merritt, *At the Crossroads: Indians & Empires on a Mid-Atlantic Frontier, 1700–1763* (Chapel Hill: University of North Carolina Press, 2003); and Geoffrey Plank, *An Unsettled Conquest: The British Campaign against the Peoples of Acadia* (Philadelphia: University of Pennsylvania Press, 2001).

4. Another incomplete list would include David Armitage, *The Ideological Origins of the British Empire* (Cambridge, U.K.: Cambridge University Press, 2000) and "The Declaration of Independence and International Law," *William and Mary Quarterly*, 3rd ser., 59 (2002): 39–64; Eliga H. Gould, "Zones of Law, Zones of Violence:

The Legal Geography of the British Atlantic, circa 1772," *William and Mary Quarterly,* 3rd ser., 60 (2003): 471–510; and Peter S. Onuf, *Jefferson's Empire: The Language of American Nationhood* (Charlottesville: University Press of Virginia, 2000), esp. chap. 2. Also see T. H. Breen's call for a greater sensitivity to the British context of the Revolution in "Ideology and Nationalism on the Eve of the American Revolution: Revisions Once More in Need of Revising," *Journal of American History* 84 (1997): 13–39.

5. Onuf, *Jefferson's Empire,* esp. 57–61; J. G. A. Pocock, "States, Republics, and Empires: The American Founding in Early Modern Perspective," in *Conceptual Change and the Constitution,* ed. Terrence J. Ball and J. G. A. Pocock (Lawrence: University Press of Kansas, 1988), esp. 66–73.

6. Jack P. Greene, *Peripheries and Centers: Constitutional Development in the Extended Polities of the British Empire and the United States 1607–1788* (Athens: University of Georgia Press, 1986), 205.

7. For a brief exploration of the question, see my "Visions of Another Empire: John Ledyard, American Traveler across the Russian Empire, 1787–88," *Journal of the Early Republic* 24 (2004): 347–80.

Continuity and Change in Early American Studies

Don Higginbotham

I want to devote my space mainly to the first of the three "disjunctions" that Maier describes as characterizing early American history today: the tendency to separate colonial and Revolutionary studies, to see them as distinct or scarcely related. This development is relatively new. In their writings and training of graduate students, few if any distinguished historians until recently practiced such compartmentalization. Here one begins with Charles Andrews, the dean of early American historians in the first three or more decades of the twentieth century. In the following generation of scholars, one thinks of Samuel Eliot Morison, Curtis Nettles, Richard B. Morris, and John R. Alden. One also calls to mind a slightly later group of practitioners, such as Bernard Bailyn and Edmund S. Morgan, both preeminent in the field. Others at or near retirement now, such as Jack P. Greene and John Murrin, also do both colonial and Revolutionary history. People entering the job market in the late 1950s, as I did, almost always found that advertisements about openings in early American history did not express a preference for candidates in pre-1763 America as opposed to post-1763, or vice versa. At my institution, the University of North Carolina at Chapel Hill, we were fortunate over many years to have two faculty positions in pre-1800 areas. For thirty-five years, my colleague John Nelson and I rotated graduate and undergraduate colonial and Revolutionary course offerings in order for both of us to keep current, as best we could, with new literature and changing interpretations.

Another way of making the point about the once-pervasive link between colonial and Revolutionary history is to look at schools of interpretation. The

From *Historically Speaking* 6 (March/April 2005)

imperial and progressive schools lost much of their influence in the post-1945 years, but they always agreed on one thing: continuity. The imperialists saw institutional and constitutional developments that were in some measure persistent throughout the eighteenth century, just as the progressives saw tensions and divisions in late colonial society that continued into the Revolution and led to the beginnings of political party development. In the 1950s the consensus academics, especially Daniel Boorstin and Louis Hartz, maintained that one could not understand the Revolution without an awareness of dynamic social and economic currents that were undermining "the old regime" well before Lexington and Concord. As much as Bailyn and Greene might dissent from the emphases of the above-mentioned schools of thought, they nonetheless have continued to make powerful arguments for colonial America—the thirteen colonies, at least—remaining overwhelmingly British in the political and cultural realms, with the British heritage hardly ceasing to be the dominant one in the Revolution and the Federalist period. To single out Greene, who admittedly is the best example, one should consult the following: his *Peripheries and Center: Constitutional Development in the Extended Polities of the British Empire and the United States, 1607–1788* (1986), *Pursuits of Happiness: The Social Development of Early Modern British Colonies and the Formation of American Culture* (1988), and, perhaps most recently, "The American Revolution," *American Historical Review* 105 (2000): 93–103. Greene, along with Murrin, sees a replication of much of metropolitan culture, a process of Anglicization, having taken place before the disruption of the first British Empire. Within limits, T. H. Breen accepts this interpretation in *The Marketplace of Revolution: How Consumer Politics Shaped American Independence* (2004), which details the huge quantity of British manufactured items acquired by vastly increasing numbers of provincial consumers and its implications for the Revolution.

My sympathies rest with Maier and Greene in raising some concerns about efforts to create a disjunction between the colonial and Revolutionary periods. The statement does not mean I have problems with the various "new" histories, some newer than others. Social history works particularly well in a British American context: for instance, the inclusion of peoples left out or mainly ignored by imperialists, consensus scholars, and other interpreters—women, Native Americans, African Americans, white urban lower orders, and so on. So, too, are Atlantic history and comparative empires applicable. I don't believe one can be a good historian by writing and teaching in any field without stressing comparative and contextual dimensions. One can hardly understand colonial British America without an awareness of how the British experience was similar or dissimilar to the encounters of France and Spain.

For example, the Atlantic Ocean explains the interconnectedness of four continents in terms of the African slave trade. Even before that human traffic significantly affected all of the New World, these three European colonizers had labor problems, which they approached in different ways. All attempted in some of their ventures to resurrect forms of European feudalism, then expiring in the Old World: the Spanish with their encomienda system, the English with their proprietary colonies, and the French with their seigneurial system, and all resulted in failures. Everywhere in North America there was a westward movement. But historians must explain why the French and Spanish quickly penetrated far into the continent and why the English for more than a century clung to the Atlantic coastline, resembling the country of Chile, to borrow from Lawrence Henry Gipson. As for the American Revolution, we can better understand its achievements if we compare it with the instability and internal tensions associated with the revolutions in Mexico and other parts of Latin America.

In fact, there is nothing new in advocating the comparative approach. That idea was eloquently presented seventy years ago by Herbert Eugene Bolton, the great scholar of the Spanish borderlands, in his *The Wider Horizons of American History* and by some of his students, including John Tate Lanning, one of my graduate teachers at Duke University. A further example is W. J. Eccles, who was the most influential Anglo-Canadian historian of New France prior to his death a few years ago. In his *Canadian Frontier* (1969), *France in America* (1972), and *Essays on New France* (1987), Eccles shed light on important comparative developments in British America—population growth, economic development, Indian affairs, and religious influences.

Maier singles out Alan Taylor's recent textbook *American Colonies* (2001) as an important example of the disjunction of early American studies. She notes that it ignores any sustained treatment of the Revolution or the connection between colonial and Revolutionary history. Up to a point, I have to defend Taylor because I am using his volume in my own colonial course! It was not his purpose to write a history of both the colonial and Revolutionary periods. Indeed, the core of this superbly written book, as one can see from most of the chapter titles, covers standard topics, but at the same time Taylor includes information from the best recent examinations of social and cultural history, and he devotes admirable space to other New World empires and to dimensions of Atlantic history. I agree with Maier that the concluding chapter on "The Pacific, 1760–1820" seems out of place in a book that, as I have indicated, focuses mainly on colonial British America. It is fair enough to avoid any extended treatment of the Revolution in a colonial text, but the references to it in the above-mentioned chapter on the Far West really seem inappropriate in the kind of book he has chosen to give us. Consequently I did not assign that concluding chapter in my colonial class.

If, as Maier observes, much of the new history represents a move away from the examination of state-formation in America, that subject is actually alive and well, and Maier is partly responsible for its survival with her own work, which now includes a study in progress on the ratification of the Constitution. It is, to be sure, of more interest to the general reading public than the new histories. Such recent portraits of the founders by David McCullough, Walter Isaacson, Ron Chernow, Edmund Morgan, Gordon S. Wood, and Joseph Ellis are in considerable part devoted to state-formation, and the last three are academic historians. We should add that McCullough, Wood, and Ellis have won Pulitzer prizes.

Both the old political history and the innovative social and cultural histories are prosperous. There is now a noticeable trend among some younger scholars and even an occasional senior historian, such as Alfred Young, to link the two by studying what might be called popular politics. They are "joining the party," even though Maier may think they are off in one corner. And let us throw in the names of Peter S. Onuf, Jack Rakove, Richard Beeman, and Rosemarie Zagarri; they have been partygoers throughout their impressive academic careers. My one concern, which I share fully with Maier, is that we be mindful of the connection between the colonial and Revolutionary periods, of the inextricable tie between continuity and change in history.

Comments on Pauline Maier's "State of the Field"

Peter S. Onuf

The drafting and ratification of the federal Constitution should be a pivotal topic in American historical studies, linking colonial and Revolutionary history. Instead, Maier complains, the "disjunction" between the two periods has been growing; with the exception of a few senior historians, only political scientists and law professors till this neglected field. But I think she exaggerates. Recent historiographical developments suggest that the disjunction is disappearing.

Before I elaborate this claim, let me briefly address the other two disjunctions Pauline emphasizes, the one "between scholarly interests and those of the reading public" and the other "between historical scholarship and history as taught in secondary school." Of course, these disjunctions have always been with us, but they don't strike me as particularly severe now. As long as I've been in the business, historians have complained about failing to reach a general audience and about how we need to "return to narrative." Yet all this time, even during the heyday of social science history, historians have been reaching a general audience. Jeremiads about our impending irrelevance have reinforced the powerful influence of best-seller lists, bicentennials, and high school curricula in shaping our agenda. Rants against American exceptionalism—the all-purpose pejorative for this pandering to the public—are themselves eloquent testimony to our continuing relevance and responsiveness. The danger is not that we will lose our readers, but that we'll end up having nothing useful or difficult or discomfiting to say to them.

Maier suggests that the profession as a whole has moved progressively—or, perhaps, regressively—"from political to social and then cultural history,"

From *Historically Speaking* 6 (March/April 2005)

taking concluding potshots at "imagined communities" and the so-called "public sphere." These missiles, to mix metaphors, seem misguided to me. Benedict Anderson and Jürgen Habermas, once fashionable, are easily caricatured these days, and it is undoubtedly the case that much silly and reductive work has been committed in their name. The complaint appears to be that big generalizations about print culture are not empirically grounded. But surely the return to politics and political culture should be welcome, particularly when historians move past print and dig deep in the sources. And students of national identity and nation-making provide a good antidote to exceptionalism—taking the "nation," its singularity, and its superiority for granted—without indulging in America-bashing (another perverse and lamentable symptom of exceptionalism) or avoiding the subject altogether. New work on nation-building and political culture is in fact addressing the very disjunction Maier laments. This work promises to liberate us at last from the reductive influence of the ideological school on our understanding of the Revolution.

Building on the neo-Whig resuscitation of political and constitutional thought, the republicanists located the real revolution in a putative ideological transformation that antedated the war itself, making mere institutional developments seem epiphenomenal. The search for deep patterns in political discourse and their remote classical origins mirrored the social historians' search for deep structures in society. Both approaches militated against political history. Both either insisted on the fundamental continuity between colonial and Revolutionary history or stipulated a Revolutionary transformation that had little or nothing to do with politics in the conventional sense. The ascendancy of the republican revisionists was thus a disaster for political history in the narrow, conventional sense. Promising beginnings to the study of Revolutionary political mobilization—including Maier's superb *From Resistance to Revolution* (1972)—could not be sustained, despite the extraordinary efforts of the new social historians to prepare the way. It was hard to take mobilization seriously when it had so little apparent connection to the deep cultural and social structural transformations that the study of political language supposedly illuminated. What was happening on the ground seemed epiphenomenal at best, and the relation between the real revolution and the military conflict itself seemed increasingly tenuous.

The problem with the revisionists' conception of ideology is that it obscures contingency and therefore the domain of political choice and action in which our subjects operated. They are instead depicted as prisoners of language, captured by a world view that blinded them to reality. Or, to put the case more modestly, the revisionists mined the discourse of the period so effectively for deeper meanings, meanings that transcended immediate circumstances, that these circumstances themselves, the world as our subjects themselves understood it, faded from view. But there are good reasons to believe that the ideological wave has at last crested and that historians are returning to the Revolution. This could only happen when scholars *stopped* taking the ideas of the Revolution (as the revisionists understood them) quite so seriously and *stopped* assuming that the evolution of political institutions was itself in any meaningful sense ideologically determined. In short, the revival of the political history of the Revolution, now in progress, depended on the ultimate exhaustion of the republican synthesis.

Recent historiographical developments are encouraging. The now-fashionable study of nationalism and national identity offers a much more modest and politically instrumental understanding of ideologies as inventions and improvisations that were necessarily responsive to actual circumstances. In retrospect, the (successful) nation is the prime site for political mystification in the modern world; in prospect, however, any given nation is at best a project, a bet against long odds, that cannot succeed without effective mass mobilization. American patriots may have begun mobilizing long before the break with Britain, but they had no clear sense of what they were mobilizing *for* or whether, when the crisis came, they would have sufficient popular support to claim some sort of legitimacy; at first, they could have no idea that they were making a nation—whatever that was. Maier's *American Scripture* (1997) is an exemplary study of the culminating phase of the mobilization process leading up to independence. She rightly emphasizes the importance of widespread local initiatives, thus focusing our attention on the importance of the particular social and political contexts that the ideological historians tended to overlook. By the same token, many communities did *not* declare their own independence, loyalists remained dominant in many parts of what became the United States, and opportunists everywhere kept their options open.

Maier's deconstruction of a monolithic Declaration (written by Thomas Jefferson on behalf of a notional American people) is a breath of fresh air, an invitation to scholars to mobilize once again for a proper study of the Revolution. But she was not working in a historiographical vacuum or wasteland when she wrote *Scripture,* nor is she doing so now in her current work on the ratification of the federal Constitution. Complementary efforts by students of civic life to move beyond—or beneath—abstract formulations of the bourgeois public sphere are also yielding promising results. (John Brooke's important essays have helped set the agenda for these efforts.) The history of specific associations, not a generalized associational impulse linked to the transformation of underlying class relations, resulted in Revolutionary political change —a point Maier made very effectively in her "Revolutionary Origins of the American Corporation" in the *William and Mary Quarterly* (1993) on the proliferation of the corporate form in post-Revolutionary America, despite the powerful republican antipathy to monopoly. Younger scholars are showing a new and salutary interest in who joined what civic groups—political, military, fraternal, religious, and charitable—and what purposes they hoped to achieve. (For a good introduction to the exciting new literature on this and other themes in the history of the early republic, see Jeffrey Pasley, Andrew Robertson, and David Waldstreicher, eds., *Beyond the Founders: New Approaches to the Political History of the Early American Republic* [2004]).

More immediately to the point of Maier's present project, new work in British imperial and Atlantic history as well as in the history of Indian Country during the Revolutionary era gives us a fresher sense of the geopolitical context and consequences of the Revolution. Ideological (and exceptionalist) navel-gazing—what sort of regime did the founders inaugurate?—is giving way to a more historicized account of how the Revolutionaries understood their world and what they hoped to accomplish. As Maier notes, Max Edling's *Revolution in Favor of Government* (2003) is a wonderful example of the interpretative payoffs of this changing perspective: whatever their ideological tendencies and preferences, the founders "wanted to form a 'fiscal-military state' like those of contemporary Europe." There was plenty of room for controversy in this state-making project, as there would be for decades to come over the character of American federalism. David Hendrickson's *Peace Pact: The Lost World of the American Founding* (2003) is a brilliant exploration of the conceptual problems of federal state-building that provides a necessary complement to the new literature on American political development. And I would emphasize here as well Jack P. Greene's *Peripheries and Center* (1986), a now-classic study that framed the federal problem in the larger context of British imperial as well as American constitutional history and thus bridged the disjunction between our understandings of the colonial and Revolutionary periods.

The time is right for Maier's study of the ratification debates. I'm mildly chiding her here for exaggerating the problems in the field in a somewhat self-serving way. The disjunction between colonial (and imperial) and early national history is not as great as she claims, and she will not be bridging it alone (or in the lonely company of senior historians who write about the founders). But Maier has always been at the forefront of our field—in her work on mobilization and the "Old Revolutionaries," in her study of Jefferson and the Declaration—and I wouldn't want to quarrel with her sense of what's missing and what's wrong with the field if it provides the rationale and impetus for still more important work.

Political History's Demise?

Paul A. Rahe

I come at the question raised by Pauline Maier from a peculiar perspective. I was trained in ancient Greek and Roman history. In graduate school I took not one course in American history, and I paid it very little attention when I was an undergraduate. I stumbled into the field more or less by accident. Unhappy with the orthodoxy then current regarding the Spartan constitution, I set out to write a thumb-sucker comparing the Spartan constitution, which I knew I did not fully understand, with the American Constitution, which I wrongly presumed was more familiar and easier for one such as myself to comprehend. I quickly discovered that modern constitutionalism is a slippery subject; my thumb-sucker ran to twelve hundred pages and took me a decade to write; and I now hold a chair in American history and teach seventeenth-century English history as well. This gives me an odd perspective on the early American field—not unlike the one recommended by Thomas Jefferson to his young correspondents, for my formal education and my subsequent self-education more or less tracks his suggestion that to be able citizens, Americans need to know the history of self-government in ancient Greece and Rome, modern England, and America.

If I had been asked ten years ago to say something concerning the field of early American political and intellectual history, I would have been ecstatic. From the 1960s through the early 1990s, there was a remarkable outpouring of books on American political thought, the American Revolution, and the American founding. Caroline Robbins, Edmund S. Morgan, Jack P. Greene, Bernard Bailyn, and Gordon S. Wood set the stage. J. G. A. Pocock proposed a grand and complex hypothesis concerning the origins and character of early American political thought. And, with funding from a variety of federal and state agencies and private foundations, a great many scholars—historians and political scientists alike—turned their attention to the evidence. At the same time, a host of editing projects made easily accessible the letters and papers of the most important figures in the period, the records of the Constitutional Convention, the writings of the Federalists and of the Anti-Federalists, and virtually every piece of evidence pertinent to the interpretation of the ratification process. The debates that ensued were vigorous and enlightening, and a generation or two of students became quite familiar with what had taken place in British North America in the period stretching from 1762 to 1800 and beyond. Within the field of early American political and intellectual history, the long bicentennial celebration was a remarkable scholarly success.

The last ten years, however, have been something else. I do not mean to say that no good work has been done, but it would be an understatement to say that the pace has dropped off. Arguably this was inevitable. To begin with, there was exhaustion. After 1990 no one was especially eager to attend yet another conference on *The Federalist,* and younger scholars quite naturally wanted to plow fields as yet untilled. Then, there is the fact that funding dried up. The bicentennial was over, and the various agencies and foundations moved on. This is, to some extent, as it should be: one cannot maintain the species of scholarly focus that existed in the bicentennial period for very long, nor should one want to.

But things are, I believe, much worse than they should be. My evidence is anecdotal, but it confirms in every particular Maier's sage observations. Indeed, everything that I have heard or read points to a single conclusion: within the history profession, there is a general turning away from early American political history and political thought. If one is a neophyte and if one wishes to make a career for oneself as an historian, one would be well advised to avoid the field.

My suspicion is that there are a great many campuses where there are no courses focused on the American Revolution and the American founding. Seven years ago I was a visiting professor at Yale University, the institution where I received my doctorate. I was asked to teach a lecture course on the American Revolution, which I was happy to work up. I was shocked to learn that no such course had been taught for a decade. A social historian had been hired to replace a political historian who had retired, and he was not interested in the Revolution. It apparently crossed no one's mind that the needs of students should come first, that what one wrote on was one thing and what one needed to teach was another.

This trend is not limited to major research universities. Again, my evidence is anecdotal, but what I have seen at my own institution and have been told of elsewhere suggests a trend: professors at smaller institutions, dedicated to the teaching of undergraduates and perhaps also to the formation of graduate students, are to an increasing degree eager to fashion sinecures for themselves, enabling them to teach little else but that on which they happen to be writing. One consequence is that the focus of teaching, even in very small departments, gets narrower with every passing year. Whole periods of American history are never taught; whole epochs of European history are barely mentioned. In our graduate programs, we seem to be training scholars, which is reason for celebration, but we also seem to be training them in such a way that they do not take their mission as teachers as seriously as they should.

I said earlier that my perspective is peculiar. I come at early American history from Greek, Roman, and early modern European history, and what I see in all those fields is a drift away from politics. If the study of history is a species of antiquarianism, this is of little importance: as human beings, we can find entertainment in a great many subjects. But in the past the study of history was thought of as part of a civic education. This was the view of Thomas Jefferson, and concerns of this sort inspired Herodotus, Thucydides, Xenophon, Cato, Sallust, Livy, Tacitus, Machiavelli, Guicciardini, Clarendon, Hume, Gibbon, Macaulay, Churchill, and, in our own day, Solzhenitsyn. Not so long ago, this was the understanding in the United States as well. And, of course, in certain circles it does persist. I wonder, however, how many courses in American history departments have statesmanship as their focus.

Let me be a bit more precise about what worries me. A couple of years ago, I was interviewed at a major research university, a gigantic public university, which was looking for a department chair. Having held that post at my own university, I was not enthusiastic at the prospect of managing a department with something like fifty members, but I agreed to take a look. What I discovered shocked me. This was a large department about to get larger: it had fourteen lines to fill. Not one of its members was a full-time military historian (an Africanist occasionally taught a course in the field), and it had no intention of adding anyone in the field. A couple of years later, a retired Russian historian from an even more distinguished department at another state university remarked to me that some years back, when he was deputy chair, his department had turned down an endowed chair in military history. The department chairperson had threatened to resign if the department accepted the chair. He was morally opposed to their teaching military history, and he was by no means alone. The truth of the matter is that military history has virtually disappeared from the American academy. There is not one university in twenty that in its history department offers courses on the origins, the conduct, and the consequences of war. Given the recent history of this country and its prospects, one would think that the history of warfare would be a focus. How can citizens exercise judgment concerning something that they have never had occasion to think seriously about?

What is true for military history is to an increasing degree true for diplomatic history as well. The latter was once a thriving field. It is, to say the least, important. But it is falling by the wayside. There are institutions—Yale University is one—that are exceptions to this rule, but they are few. Take a look at the journals dedicated to particular historical periods. Look over the list of panels at the national meetings, and you will see that, to an increasing degree, diplomatic history is absent. Again, if our focus is the formation of citizens, this is deeply disturbing: citizens who have not studied statesmanship with regard to peace and war will be ill equipped to judge the statesmanship of their leaders.

Unless I am mistaken, political history is not far behind. How many universities today offer courses on the English, French, and Russian revolutions? In how many places is the evolution of parliamentary government a focus? British historians tell me that in the United States, English constitutional history is a dying field. I hear the like from Renaissance historians. If so, general trends would help explain the apparent decline in the number of scholars working on or even teaching the American founding.

I do not mean to denigrate the work done by social and economic historians, but I do assert the centrality of political history understood in the broadest possible sense. The other fields are in the end ancillary. Their greatest value lies in the contribution they make to political understanding, which is, let me underline, very considerable. One need only consider the manner in which slavery shaped the early American republic to see just how much social and economic historians can teach political historians. My worry is that we have forgotten what is central and what is ancillary, that we are rapidly descending into an aimless antiquarianism, and that we are denying our students the tools that they desperately need if they are to function effectively and intelligently as citizens.

Let me pose a question at the end. Why is it that the profession seems increasingly in the grips of a hostility to politics? We do not hire military historians because we regard their interests as distasteful. To an increasing degree, we regard diplomatic historians in the same fashion. After all, they, too, are interested in the projection of power. Will political history soon be a field that "decent people" will not touch?

An Agenda for Early American History

Jack N. Rakove

Scholars of a certain age, when asked to reflect on the state of their field, are entitled to wax autobiographical, so I begin by recalling my own association with Pauline Maier. When I started graduate school at Harvard University in 1969, she was an assistant professor at the University of Massachusetts, Boston. Her first book, *From Resistance to Revolution,* came out as I was starting my dissertation and helped shaped some of the questions I asked in its opening chapters. We had carrels in the same quarantined zone of Widener Library where typing was permitted and where we chatted about our common interests, like making sense of Samuel Adams. (I trace the origins of my own dissertation to a casual remark that our mutual mentor, Bernard Bailyn, once made to me over lunch: if you could explain what Adams was up to, you might account for 30 percent of the causation of the American Revolution. Without yet knowing what multiple regression was, that number seemed big enough to warrant further thought.) A third of a century (and now many e-mails) later, our interests still overlap; she is working on the Constitution, as I have, and I am doing a book called *Revolutionaries* (not wholly unlike her second book, *The Old Revolutionaries*). Both of us are trying to bridge the gap between scholarship and lay readership that is the topic of her second "disjunction," in the process shedding our common editor and publisher, hiring literary agents, and testing the market in a way that would have seemed inconceivable during the Nixon years.

It should not surprise, therefore, that I respond favorably to most of Maier's assessment of the state of early American history. The substantive points that matter most, I believe, are those concerned with her first disjunction, between the primarily social and cultural character of scholarship

From *Historically Speaking* 6 (March/April 2005)

addressed to the colonial era proper, and the avowedly political emphases of the study of the Revolution.

To start out as an early Americanist in the early 1970s was bliss. Both parts of the field were hot. The demographic studies of New England communities were just appearing, followed within a few years by a surge of similar work on the Chesapeake, as well as Peter H. Wood's pathbreaking study of slavery in South Carolina, *Black Majority*. Nor was the study of colonial politics a neglected area. For my orals, I probably read a good twenty monographs on the politics of individual colonies—not the old institutional stuff against which the original progressive historians had been reacting but recent works with strong interpretive motifs by people like Gary B. Nash and Stanley Katz.

But in the realm of politics, the real action lay within the Revolution, which is why I foreswore my original interest in recent American history and moved back two centuries. It mattered a great deal of course that Bailyn's *Ideological Origins of the American Revolution* had just appeared in its original two incarnations (as the introduction to that lonely initial volume of *Pamphlets of the American Revolution* and then separately as a book). Then there was the stream of monographs by Gordon S. Wood, Richard D. Brown, Jere Daniell, Mary Beth Norton, and, of course, Pauline Maier. In this context, it seemed entirely plausible that an old, tried and true, seemingly exhausted subject like the Continental Congress might actually be ripe for reexamination.

As I assess the state of the field three decades later, I can offer at least three main judgments. First, and easiest, the study of colonial politics, as it was conceived then, is dead. If there are important aspects of the history of American political development to be located in the colonial era, one would not know it from the historical literature. But the new interest in the nature of empires and imperialism, which can be seen as a collateral branch of Atlantic history, has opened up a more expansive way of thinking about the structure of politics and the nature of governance.

Second, (as Maier, in passing, quotes me as observing), I think the reinterpretation of the American Revolution that was heralded by Edmund S. Morgan and Helen M. Morgan's seminal study of *The Stamp Act Crisis* (1953) and then propelled by the work of Bailyn and his students in the late 1960s and 1970s has largely solved the major causal problems of explaining why the Revolution occurred. I know this judgment sounds presumptuous to the point of arrogance. But it may also offer a useful way of explaining why an account that emphasizes the fundamentally constitutional and political nature of the controversy has survived intact and largely unchallenged for a quarter century now. Other questions remain to be asked about the period after 1776 and the constitutional and political transformations of the 1780s and 1790s, but the question of how the colonists moved (in Maier's language) from resistance to revolution has been largely answered, demonstrating that there is indeed such a thing as progress in historical knowledge.

But the study and interpretation of the Revolutionary era cannot be confined solely to the task of explaining why the Revolution occurred. Or to put the point another way: getting from 1765 (or some other date) to 1776 is only one component—fundamental but not comprehensive—of a larger and more complicated story that has yet to be told. This larger story involves at least two other major lines of inquiry where much remains to be done. The first of these concerns what the Revolution meant to ordinary Americans—whether classified as individual participants, residents of communities, or members of some other identifiable groups (defined in terms of gender, occupation, religion or ethnicity or race, and the like)—once it was launched. Here I think it is important to distinguish clearly between the origins of the event, which can be satisfactorily explained, as I've already indicated, in political-constitutional terms, and the meaning(s) the Revolution acquired for everyone who was caught up in the prolonged war that ensued, with all the opportunities and dislocations it generated. We have only scratched the surface of what is possible and indeed needed on this front.

The second line of inquiry returns to the political consequences of independence. Maier notes the impact on her own thinking of Max Edling's fine monograph reinterpreting the origins of the Constitution more as a Hamiltonian exercise in state-building than a Madisonian attempt to cure the mischief of factious republicanism. One could also mention the political scientist David Hendrickson's *Peace Pact*, which seems to echo the brothers Onuf in treating the American federal project as an alternative to the Old World system of maintaining a balance of power among fully sovereign nation-states. I have some reservations about pushing this comparison too far, primarily because I wonder whether the individual American states, if disunited, would ever have been able to muster the resources and manpower to threaten each other. But there is no question that this new attention to state-building and the political economy of federalism is already inspiring a creative reconsideration of the deeper political and intellectual context of American constitutionalism. It can build upon the studies of how Americans mobilized to wage the Revolutionary War, such as Richard Buel's *Dear Liberty* and *In Irons* and Wayne Bodle's account in *The Valley Forge Winter*. More than that, this new interest in the making of the federal state system also provides potentially valuable links to both the imperial dimension of Atlantic history and the vicissitudes of the first quarter century of national governance under the Constitution. For those of us who think that politics is finally about who wields power—to what end and with what consequences—this approach promises a greater payoff than the recent spate of books on the political culture of the early republic, stimulating as those have been in their own way.

My third and last judgment has to do with that vast realm of social and cultural history covering the colonial era. I have always enjoyed teaching this part of the larger field, even though my research interests lie elsewhere—but my active engagement with it has grown more limited over the years, a function of the constraints of Stanford University's quarter system and the development of other teaching interests.

The one set of issues I find most interesting in this area revolves around the role of entrepreneurship and raw acquisitiveness in the process of colonial settlement and development. It is the topic I now find myself stressing in the readings I assign my graduate students. I insist they read Thomas Doerflinger's *Vigorous Spirit of Enterprise* because its discussion of entrepreneurial risk-taking forces them to consider basic questions that few historians seriously confront. Similarly I like to have them consider the tension that Bailyn establishes in *Voyagers to the West* between the visions of sugar plums dancing in land speculators' heads and the very different motives that characterize the two main types of migration that Bailyn describes. If we had enough time, I would like them to read all of Charles Royster's droll history of the Dismal Swamp Company. I have become more and more convinced that we cannot understand the nature of colonial society without entering sympathetically as well as critically into the world and ambitions of the merchants and speculators and large land (and slave) owners who were best situated to undertake the initiatives that shaped colonial society. And insofar as the tendency of the 1960s and 1970s to treat social history as a story from the bottom up has given way to the cultural historians' propensity to view the world from the margins out, I wonder how well either we or our students understand the nature of the economic ambitions that were central to the whole colonizing enterprise.

Rejoinder

Pauline Maier

The first of my "disjunctions"—between scholarship on colonial America and on the American Revolution—provoked more discussion in these thoughtful comments than anything else I said. Although I carefully stated that I was merely noting—not criticizing—that disjunction, some respondents inferred that I was complaining about it or found it frustrating. In fact, the tendency toward interpreting colonial America more broadly than the original thirteen colonies makes considerable intellectual sense. It avoids the obvious anachronism in defining the subject in terms of a future identity that most colonists did not foresee and wanted above all to avoid. But a colonial America defined as a history of all the peoples of North America or as part of the Atlantic world does not easily connect with the more nation-based study of the American Revolution.

A disjunction in historical scholarship is not, however, a disjunction in history. Nobody since Thomas Paine has, I think, seriously argued that time began anew in 1776, such that all previous history could simply be forgotten. To put it another way, Edward Gray's dream of a time when "questions about the creation of the United States cannot be divorced from important questions about the colonies" has long since been fulfilled. The profound penetration of a British identity beyond the political order into virtually every aspect of colonial life that Gray mentions is precisely what made independence so difficult to accept. Even a quick survey of debates in the Constitutional Convention shows how much delegates remained ex-colonists: both those who cited British precedents and those who denied their relevance testified to the continuing presence of the imperial past in American minds. Moreover, as Don Higginbotham notes, there exists a substantial older literature on the colonial background of the American Revolution. Those of us who teach and write on the Revolution can and do draw on that work—as well as some more recent books, such as Jon Butler's *Becoming American: The Revolution before 1776* (2000), which I probably ought to have mentioned.

The current interest in empire might, as Peter Onuf suggests, lead scholars toward "a fresher sense of the geopolitical context and consequences of the Revolution." But will it weaken or destroy the disjunction between scholarship on colonial America and that on the Revolution, as Gray and Onuf claim? I remain skeptical. The former field seems firmly committed to a broad geographical scope, while the latter will probably remain for the most part an event-laden episode in national history even when enriched by a broader comparative context. Certainly the books by Max Edling and David Hendrickson that Onuf cites focus on American state-building and fail to bridge the colonial and Revolutionary periods unless, as Onuf surprisingly asserts in his first sentence, the drafting and ratification of the Constitution —not 1776 or even the peace of 1783—should be seen as linking those periods. The only book he mentions that ties the colonial period—as conventionally understood—to the Revolution is Jack Greene's *Peripheries and Center*, which was published almost two decades ago.

I cannot resist questioning Onuf's historiographical summary and analysis. The discovery of the Revolution's ideological origins, as I witnessed it as a Harvard graduate student, allowed historians to see events through eighteenth-century eyes and so constituted a major victory in the struggle against anachronism that lies at the heart of good history. Moreover, it did not suggest that politics and political institutions were ideologically determined. Patriots and Loyalists, after all, drew different conclusions from the same Whig assumptions; and although the broad popular base of both extralegal and, later, constitutional government owed much to Whig ideology, institutional forms nonetheless provoked prolonged and lively debate. The "republican synthesis" can be safely forgotten along with its obsession with "virtue," based as it was on a very selective reading of the documentary record. We cannot, however, stop taking ideas seriously without taking a major step backward in historical understanding. Jack Rakove is nearer the truth, I think, when he says that scholars of the 1960s and 1970s—who built on the rediscovery of Revolutionary ideology—produced a "fundamentally constitutional and political" account of the Revolution that has survived "intact and largely unchallenged" for a quarter century.

And what of Onuf's dismissal of my second and third disjunctions— between the interests of the reading public and younger scholars and between directions in scholarship and the needs of high school teachers and college professors who teach the U.S. survey—as nothing new or nonexistent? I suspect his perspective is shaped by his presence at the University of Virginia, one of a small handful of graduate institutions where early American political history is alive and well. Paul Rahe's comments on the disappearance of military and diplomatic as well as political history from university curricula confirm that a problem exists and that it has disquieting civic implications. There's nothing wrong with social and cultural history, which have proven to be fruitful fields for historical investigation. But is history a zero-sum game? Must we forget parts of the past while studying others? Shouldn't historians synthesize and perpetuate the contributions of previous scholars—at least in the classroom—while adding to the body of inherited knowledge?

In the end, however, I suspect the surprising attention given to my NEH keynote speech here and elsewhere has relatively little to do with the substance of what I said. The talk gave historians an opportunity to reflect on large historical trends that we experience but rarely discuss. Sessions at historical conferences usually examine the work of young scholars; even state-of-the-field sessions seldom feature senior scholars with the range of knowledge and depth of experience that shaped contributions to this forum. The NEH officially convened its conference last April so early American historians could instruct its staff members on current scholarship, but I suspect the real beneficiaries were historians. For that gift we should be, and are, as always, grateful to our friends at the NEH.

PART 2

The Colonial Period

Richard Hakluyt's Problem

Peter C. Mancall

In the 1580s Richard Hakluyt had a problem. After learning from his namesake cousin (known to scholars as Richard Hakluyt the elder) about what could be found in exotic lands far from Europe, he came to the conclusion that the English needed to get involved in overseas exploration and colonization. He feared it might already be too late. The Spanish had been profiting from their American enterprises for almost a century, and the Portuguese and French had also been more active than the English in transatlantic endeavors. To be sure, the Tudors had made some important efforts since Europeans heard about Christopher Columbus's voyages. The Cabots had ventured to North America in the 1490s, and Martin Frobisher had led three expeditions into the North Atlantic in the 1570s in search of the Northwest Passage. But by the 1580s the English had almost nothing to show for these efforts. Worse still, many feared that continental Europeans were spreading Catholicism in the Americas, thereby threatening the Protestant English, who also resented the growing wealth of their Iberian rivals. Given the apparent unwillingness of the English to do more than occasionally support ventures to the Americas, how was Hakluyt—a man who never traveled farther from England than to Paris—going to convince them that they could wait no longer? As Americans in 2007 mark the four hundredth anniversary of the founding of Jamestown, the time seems ripe to explore how Hakluyt solved his problem and helped usher in the English colonization of North America.

In retrospect, it takes no great expertise to understand why the English should have embraced colonization. By the middle of the sixteenth century, they had become aware of the great profits that the Spanish in particular were extracting from the Americas. By the mid-1570s some English observers had concluded that the realm was overcrowded and that mobs of young underemployed or unemployed men threatened the social order. The prevailing way to deal with that crisis was to try miscreants for thefts against property and then sentence them to death. In that decade, Sir Humphrey Gilbert, a brutal military commander who took no pity on Irish Catholics during an invasion authorized by Queen Elizabeth I, suggested that it would be better to send these surplus individuals to new colonies. But it was not only such pragmatic concerns that came to matter to many. Reports of purported atrocities committed by conquistadors against indigenous Americans angered many of the English, who believed such actions revealed deep flaws of a Catholic Church bent on expansion regardless of the human costs. Longstanding desires to increase the profits to the queen, find the still-elusive Northwest Passage, extract wealth from the Americas, and spread Reformed (Protestant) Christianity also fueled the desire for colonies.

The trick is not describing the *why* of colonization but instead *how* these ideas came to motivate actual exploratory and colonial ventures. Hakluyt, more than any other individual in the realm in the late sixteenth century, figured out how to turn English policy makers and merchants into dedicated colonizers. He did so by gathering, editing, and printing travel accounts in order to demonstrate that the English had a tradition of traveling abroad and to inform his readers about what they could find if they joined an expedition. In the process, he found ways to move expansionary efforts from theory to practice.

By the early 1580s, Hakluyt realized what many historians have long since concluded: if the English were ever going to colonize North America, they were going to need to find a way to mount a sustained transatlantic effort without the kinds of direct state intervention that had propelled the Spanish toward their dominance in territory encompassing the Caribbean basin, Mexico, Central America, and northern South America. Queen Elizabeth I felt expansionist impulses, as she demonstrated with her efforts to conquer Ireland. But she had not yet embraced what we might call the Atlantic paradigm: the recognition that the greatest profits awaited those willing to travel much farther than across the Irish Sea.

But what, exactly, would motivate the English? It was not as if they lacked knowledge of the wider world. After all, sixteenth-century Europeans were accustomed to reading or hearing accounts of journeys to fabulous places. Travelers had long returned with tales of great riches to be found abroad. Of course, some of them also told about the unusual people they met. The master of that genre was the English knight Sir John Mandeville, whose fourteenth-century account of his purported travels to the East was familiar to the community of scholars and policy makers in England. Many of Mandeville's claims were preposterous. Were there really people somewhere in the world who had only a hole for a mouth and consumed all of their nutrients with a straw? Could there be an entire race of people who spent the day lying on their backs and shielding their eyes from the sun with a single enormous foot? Yet despite the incredible nature of many of Mandeville's assertions, his text remained the most popular travel narrative in Europe. Over three hundred manuscript versions created before 1500 still survive, written not only in widely known languages (like French, German, and Latin) but also in more obscure tongues, such as Irish and Czech. The text remained popular even with the advent of the printing press and the explosion of new travel accounts pouring out of European publishers' houses during the sixteenth century.

Mandeville's report survived in all likelihood because those who read it or heard it read aloud by others found it entertaining despite their doubts of its accuracy about the world beyond Europe's shores. Hakluyt himself was something of a fan or at least appreciated that the narrative had some value, which he demonstrated when he included it in a major collection of travel narratives he printed in London in 1589. (Hakluyt dropped the text from a later edition, suggesting that by the end of the century he had lost faith in whatever virtues he had earlier seen in the book.) Still, even when he printed it, Hakluyt was suspicious of its veracity and told his readers so. Mandeville's text was valuable because it showed the efforts of an Englishman abroad, but it was sufficiently incredible that Hakluyt felt a warning was in order.

Hakluyt was no doubt aware that travelers often exaggerated and in many instances dissembled. This was precisely the point that the great French essayist Michel de Montaigne recognized in his essay about cannibalism in Brazil, which he had written sometime between 1578 and 1580. Montaigne was trying to figure out whether claims of Tupinamba man-eating were accurate, and this led him to offer an opinion about what kinds of authorities should be trusted. He came to the conclusion that a clever observer would be the most likely to lie. "They never show you things as they are, but bend and disguise them according to the way they have seen them," he wrote, "and to give credence to their judgment and attract you to it, they are prone to add something to their matter, to stretch it out and amplify it."[1] It was better to have a simpleminded witness provide an account because such an individual, including the traveler Montaigne relied on for his report on Brazil, lacked the imagination to embellish the facts.

For Hakluyt to propel colonization forward, he had to do more than circulate travel accounts. He first had to convince the English that he was telling them the truth about what they would find when they traveled abroad. This became a crucial part of his larger problem. Only by convincing the queen, her advisors, and influential members of the public that he was to be trusted could he hope to advance what he believed were the highest goals of the realm.

Hakluyt's solution was simple: he would publish what he believed were truthful accounts of foreign lands produced by English travelers with the idea that such narratives would inspire other English travelers and merchants. Since he had spent much of the 1570s in Oxford studying geography and reading books in six European languages, he was in a perfect position to advance his plan. In 1582 he edited a small collection of travel narratives, which he called *Divers Voyages touching the discoverie of America and the Ilands adjacent*. He hoped that by printing a series of accounts describing the Americas and earlier English claims to parts of the Western Hemisphere, he might be able to inspire others to invest in overseas expeditions. In order to strengthen his case, he emphasized that the English already had a right to much of North America based on the earlier discoveries by the Cabots. To bolster his argument, he cited the opinion of Giovanni Battista Ramusio, the greatest Venetian geographer of the sixteenth century, who had earlier testified to the Cabots' exploits and hence gave intellectual support to any Tudor efforts to stake out ownership of at least part of North America.

After the publication of *Divers Voyages*, Hakluyt received two new opportunities: Sir Humphrey Gilbert offered him space on an expedition to Newfoundland, and the queen's advisor Sir Francis Walsingham asked him to go to Paris to gather more information about European adventures to the Americas. Had he gone with Gilbert, he would have gotten the firsthand knowledge he valued so highly and presumably have come home an even more reliable authority—if he came home, that is. (Hakluyt's reading had made him acutely aware of the dangers of long ocean passages.) On the other hand, if he accepted Walsingham's invitation, he knew that his views about American opportunities would reach the queen. He chose the latter course and in 1583 sailed to Paris to take up a position as chaplain for the English ambassador. In the meantime, Gilbert took a learned young Hungarian poet named Stephen Parmenius, who was a friend of Hakluyt's, to America. Tragically the ship with Parmenius aboard sank off Newfoundland, and Gilbert himself drowned when his vessel went down on the return home.

During his time in Paris, Hakluyt wrote an elaborate promotional tract known now as "The Discourse on Western Planting." This long manuscript —it was not published until the nineteenth century—summarized Hakluyt's views of the myriad benefits to be gained from colonization, emphasized that the English needed to get to North America before other Europeans' efforts converted too many natives to Catholicism, and provided detailed instructions about the kinds of artisans and goods English vessels needed to transport across the ocean. Upon his return to England, Hakluyt presented the document to the queen. While it would be too much to claim that the "Discourse" was responsible for the four English efforts to colonize Roanoke, Virginia, from 1584 to 1588, the English after 1584 embraced the Atlantic paradigm as Hakluyt had outlined it. Further, their initial goals in their colonies followed the logic that Hakluyt himself laid out, first in the Paris document and then in his major collection of travel accounts published in 1589, *The Principall Navigations, Voiages, and Discoveries of the English Nation*.

Roanoke failed, but Hakluyt remained active in promoting the English colonization of North America and in encouraging other kinds of overseas ventures. At century's end, he produced his masterpiece, the expanded version of the *Principall Navigations,* which now filled three enormous folio volumes. He also began to advise the East India Company. When a group of merchants fitted out three ships bound for Virginia in late 1606, Hakluyt was in all likelihood the prime author of the plans for how the settlers should act once they landed on American shores. For his efforts, Hakluyt was awarded two shares of stock in the Virginia Company and offered the chance to accompany the mission. He took the shares and held them for the rest of his life, but he turned down the invitation.

The fact that Hakluyt's views prevailed raises an important question: why did his readers, including Queen Elizabeth I, trust this man who never laid eyes on the Western Hemisphere? The trick lay in presenting himself as an astute judge of any report's veracity. Hakluyt gained his readers' trust by convincing them that he made serious efforts to sort out fact from fiction in the works that he produced for the queen's advisors and the reading public. He did not hide potential problems, and he excised materials—such as Mandeville's text—that came to seem too suspicious. As the late historian David Beers Quinn noticed, Hakluyt even edited a line out of an early report about Roanoke that compared North America to paradise. He was not interested in promotion for promotion's sake. There was no point in spinning fantasies about distant places that would prove to be lies when travelers arrived, because those same travelers would eventually return to England and invariably tell others that Hakluyt was a fraud. Rather than motivate colonization by lying about what could be found abroad, Hakluyt believed that the way to move his nation to action was to become an authority to be trusted and to use that trust to advance the goals of the state. His efforts to promote the publication of other scholars' work in Spanish, Latin, German, and French revealed that he was also a man of science who would not let his desire to promote English expansion interfere with the pursuit of knowledge. Those efforts demonstrated his commitment to spreading truth even when doing so had no benefit for the English.

There was no comparable figure to Hakluyt for other sixteenth-century European nations, though the Italian humanist Peter Martyr (Pietro Martire d'Anghiera) did chronicle Columbus's efforts, and many other European reports about the Americas also arrived in Europe. But then again, no other European nation needed a Hakluyt. In those states, especially in Spain (and to a lesser extent in Portugal and France), monarchs early on saw the value of gaining American territory, and they organized efforts to claim it. The English were the exception—not only in organizing themselves so much later than the others but also in the role that the monarch played in actual colonial enterprises. Elizabeth I and her successor James I and VI needed to be convinced that expansion across the ocean made sense. Once they reached that point, they allowed merchants to organize efforts to settle lands that the monarchs recognized as belonging to the realm. Hakluyt's writings loomed large in their decisions to support colonization schemes.

During the opening years of the seventeenth century, the English decided it was worth keeping the settlement at Jamestown, Virginia, alive despite the fact that its early years were so disastrous for those who made it across the ocean. The continued support for the struggling settlement represented a substantial shift in English views toward overseas opportunities. By the end of the first decade of the new century, the English had become committed to the Atlantic paradigm. By solving his own problem—by convincing others that he was an expert whose opinions should be followed and by articulating a colonial logic that the English found compelling—Hakluyt believed he had advanced the fortunes of the realm. As it turned out, the colonies did not develop exactly along lines he imagined. But it was the fact of their development that mattered. Hakluyt helped to get the English across the ocean and convinced them that investment in overseas settlements was vital. That proved to be enough to keep the English in the colonization business.

NOTE

1. Michel de Montaigne, "Of Cannibals," in *The Complete Essays of Montaigne*, trans. Donald M. Frame (Palo Alto, Calif.: Stanford University Press, 1958), 152.

Jamestown Redivivus

An Interview with James Horn

Conducted by Randall J. Stephens

James Horn is O'Neill Director of the John D. Rockefeller Jr. Library at the Colonial Williamsburg Foundation and lecturer at the College of William and Mary. He is the author of numerous books and articles on colonial America, including *Adapting to a New World: English Society in the Seventeenth-Century Chesapeake* (University of North Carolina Press, 1994). A social historian, Horn has analyzed colonial society within the broader context of the seventeenth-century Anglophone world. He is also the editor of the just-published Library of America's edition of John Smith's works. His most recent work is *A Land as God Made It: Jamestown and the Birth of America* (Basic Books, 2005). *Historically Speaking* associate editor Randall J. Stephens spoke with Horn in October 2006.

RANDALL STEPHENS: How prominent is Jamestown in the American popular imagination?

JAMES HORN: The history of Jamestown has been almost completely overshadowed by the history of Plymouth. If you took a straw poll, I bet you'd probably find that whereas most Americans have heard of the Mayflower and the Pilgrims, far fewer would know much, if anything, about Jamestown.

STEPHENS: Did nineteenth-century American historians have something to do with this?

HORN: I trace it back to the late eighteenth century. Sectional rivalries, particularly between Virginia and Massachusetts, existed already in the 1780s. But, of course, the Civil War was what really clinched it for New England. As a consequence of the South losing the war, the New England founding myth became established as the nation's beginning, taught to millions of school children in their textbooks and celebrated annually at Thanksgiving. The victors tend to write the dominant version of history, and so Jamestown was largely forgotten.

STEPHENS: Yet the story of Pocahontas and John Smith seems to occupy an important place in the American imagination.

HORN: Absolutely. But it seems to me that the story of Smith and Pocahontas is somewhat divorced from Jamestown. The location is early Virginia, but the theme is a romance that has little to do with reality. Pocahontas was only eleven or twelve when they first met. Smith was not in love with her, and she was not in love with him. The true story of Pocahontas, at least as far as the English were concerned, is one of redemption. The fact that she converted to Christianity and joined the Anglican Church was evidence (the English believed) that Indians could be redeemed and brought to the true faith as well as, in time, to English ways. An overlooked aspect of early Virginia was the genuine effort on the part of the English to convert Indians to Christianity. It is a misconception to see Massachusetts as the "religious" colony and Virginia as the "greedy" colony.

STEPHENS: What are some other misconceptions about Jamestown?

HORN: It is a mistake to see Jamestown as a failure. Jamestown did not fail; it survived and was ultimately successful. Jamestown's survival was partly a result of the determined efforts of the settlers and the support of the Virginia Company of London, the colony's sponsor, and partly a matter of luck. But the fact that it *did* survive had consequences for the rest of the colonial period and ultimately, I'd say, for the later development of the United States.

STEPHENS: What kinds of consequences?

HORN: Think about what might have happened had Jamestown collapsed. If the English had abandoned the Chesapeake region, would Plymouth have been settled? Prior to their arrival in North America, the Pilgrims were involved in negotiations with the Virginia Company, from whom they received permission to settle in the northern part of the colony, near the Hudson River. Similarly, would the founders of the Massachusetts Bay Colony have gone to New England if there hadn't already been an English presence in the mid-Atlantic? After all, there were already French settlers in New England in the early years of the seventeenth century, but they were wiped out by an English warship coming up from Jamestown in 1613. There is no guarantee that the English would have been successful in establishing settlements elsewhere along the North American coast if Jamestown had not survived. I do not see the settlement of New England as entirely independent of what took place in Virginia.

Then there are Jamestown's enduring legacies: It was at Jamestown that English people first came into sustained contact with other peoples. They had encountered Indians before, and they had encountered Africans on the West Coast of Africa, but it was at Jamestown where the English, Indians, and Africans began living together side by side. There were tragic aspects to these encounters, which we have to recognize and come to terms with. Hostilities between the English and Powhatan Indians were merely the first in a vicious cycle of war, plunder, and exploitation—repeated over and over again across the continent during the next two and a half centuries—by which Europeans took possession of the land and dispossessed its native peoples.

To maximize profits and increase production, planters required a regular supply of laborers who could be forcibly controlled. The arrival of two dozen Africans (Angolans) at Jamestown in 1619 presaged the beginning of a system of exploitation and oppression that blighted the lives of countless Africans and their African American descendants over the next two and half centuries. But Jamestown matters precisely because it is about coming to terms with our shared past—a past painful and conflicted but that ultimately laid the foundations of modern America.

The nature of our society today owes in large measure to the foundation and survival of Jamestown, which led to the emergence of British America and the United States. It is why we speak English; it is why we have laws and political institutions based on British institutions. Virginia evolved into the most populous and wealthiest mainland colony in British America. It led the thirteen colonies into revolution and had an enormous impact on the new nation. Four of the first five presidents were Virginians.

At Jamestown, the hard lessons were learned about how to establish a successful colony. A colony could not survive as a military garrison but needed to establish private property, a profitable commodity, and some kind of representative government as well as stable social foundations. These lessons were learned at Jamestown, and certainly the Pilgrims and the Puritans were well aware of them. That was why Captain John Smith wrote several books in the 1620s: to spell out the rules for establishing a successful colony.

Finally, at Jamestown we have the first expressions of the American Dream. The reason why English settlers moved to Virginia was to make a better life for themselves, and they kept coming despite the hardships. More English settlers moved to Virginia in the seventeenth century than any other mainland colony, far more than went to New England or the Middle Colonies, for example. John Smith was the apostle of the American Dream: the vision that with hard work and thrift ordinary people could prosper and find the kind of life in America that would have been impossible at home.

STEPHENS: Did John Smith have contact with any of the people who came to New England?

HORN: Oh yes. He explored New England in 1614 and, as you might know, was responsible for naming it New England. In some ways, he became as much—if not more—of an advocate for New England as for Virginia in his later years. He had hoped to be part of the Pilgrims' expedition to Plymouth but was passed over for Miles Standish. Nevertheless, he remained convinced that trade, particularly fishing, was the way to create stable communities as well as profits both for the colonies and for England.

He was right in principle, but he got the wrong commodity. Although fish was and has continued to be an important product, the two great staples of the colonial period were tobacco and sugar. But he was surely right about the importance of trade. If ordinary people were enabled to work for their own profit and well-being, then colonies would thrive.

STEPHENS: A fascinating episode of PBS's *Scientific American Frontiers*, "Unearthing Secret America" (2002), covered Jamestown's rich archaeological record. Apparently the early settlers were far more productive than historians have thought.

HORN: Yes, the evidence contradicts the long-held view—expressed, for example, in Edmund S. Morgan's hugely influential *American Slavery, American Freedom*—that early Jamestown was run by a group of lazy English gentlemen, which resulted in starvation, disease, and death. Archaeologist Bill Kelso has found a good deal of evidence that shows just how hard the colonists were working, including, I think, the gentry. It is true that the gentry were primarily involved in exploration to find elusive gold mines or a passage to the South Sea, but they were also very active in Jamestown trying to find and grow products to send back to England.

STEPHENS: Where were most of the settlers of Jamestown from?

HORN: The majority, both in the early years and throughout the seventeenth century, would have come from London and surrounding regions. The Southeast was the most populous part of England, and that is where much of the recruiting of indentured servants took place. But there was a fair number from the West Country, who headed out from Bristol and other local ports.

STEPHENS: What would have struck them as strange and surprising about Virginia?

HORN: They would have been impressed, as they came into the Chesapeake Bay, by the size of the rivers. The bay itself is huge compared to English waterways. The English Channel, for example, is about twenty-two miles wide—the entrance to the Chesapeake Bay is almost as large. They would have also been impressed, too, by the woodlands and forests and the Indian peoples living in those areas. The English referred to their settlements as "English ground," which I think was fairly specific in distinguishing them from Indian towns. They might have glimpsed, too, working in the tobacco fields men and women brought from Africa, which might have been their first sight of slaves.

Then they would have been struck by the absence of the familiar. There were no great cities or bustling market towns, no fine gentry houses or great cathedrals. No ancient Norman church towers pierced Virginia's skies. The colony lacked the complexity and density of English society, the social gradations and centuries-old traditions and customs that regulated everyday life.

STEPHENS: I was not aware until I read your book how important the "lost colony" of Roanoke was to the early settlers of Jamestown.

HORN: The people involved in the early history of English colonization, including Roanoke, were looking for silver, gold, gems, and a passage to the South Sea. The "lost colonists," if they survived, would have been living with the Indian peoples in the interior for nearly two decades. The Jamestown settlers figured that the survivors of the Roanoke expedition would have had a pretty good idea as to the location of those gold or silver mines or whether there was in fact a passage to the South Sea. So the efforts to locate Roanoke survivors were not just recovery expeditions; there were very tangible reasons why they wanted to find them.

STEPHENS: Do you think the lost colonists merged with Native Americans?

HORN: Yes. I think the only way they could have survived was by joining local peoples. I am certain that is what happened.

STEPHENS: I read recently that you were working on a book on Roanoke. What drew you to the topic?

HORN: The story of Roanoke, like that of Jamestown, is much misunderstood. As I researched Jamestown and got into some of the issues concerning Roanoke, I realized that I simply couldn't agree with the standard view of what happened to the lost colonists. It is also, like Jamestown, a great story.

STEPHENS: What is the standard view?

HORN: The conventional theory is that when the lost colonists left Roanoke Island, they moved to the south bank of the James River and settled with Indians somewhere near the mouth of the Chesapeake Bay. The reason that this has been the dominant theory is simply that this was where they were originally heading when the expedition set out in 1587 under the leadership of John White. They were meant to go to the Chesapeake, and they got dumped on Roanoke Island instead. But I think that all the evidence points to them moving directly westward. They moved up Albemarle Sound to the confluence of the Roanoke and Chowan rivers, and that is where they established themselves initially. The idea was that they were going to wait for John White to return with extra supplies and other settlers, but, of course, he never showed up.

STEPHENS: How would he know where they were? How would they reach him?

HORN: Well, the great thing here is that there are lots of mysteries, which is what I want to write about. Why didn't they simply tell him before he left where they were going? They said they would move fifty miles inland, which suggests that they weren't quite sure where they were going to go. They left a message on Roanoke Island—the famous carving on the tree—to go to the nearby island called Croatoan. I believe that they planned to leave a small group on Croatoan, who, when White came back, would lead him to the others. They couldn't stay on Roanoke Island because the Spanish knew they were there, and local Indians were hostile. Nobody knows for certain where they went, but I think there is good evidence that suggests they ended up in the interior of North Carolina.

STEPHENS: How would this alter our basic ideas about early settlement?

HORN: It plays out in the way Virginia might have developed, which was quite different from the way it did develop. The Virginia we know, and the Chesapeake we know, are really the creation in large part of John Smith and the vision of the colony based around the Chesapeake Bay. The vision of Virginia in 1609 was quite different; it was a colony, which would stretch across the interior of North Carolina and up to the fall of the James River. It was a colony that was not based on the Chesapeake Bay but somewhat to the south and inland. Had that happened, we may have seen a different development of English settlement in this part of America. It could have been that the English would not have turned to tobacco. It is quite possible that that colony in the interior of North Carolina and Virginia would not have lasted very long because it just couldn't have kept going. They would not have found gold or a passage to the South Sea, and it would have just fizzled out.

Re-Bunking the Pilgrims

Jeremy Dupertuis Bangs

In grade school in the 1950s, I learned that the Pilgrims were the most important and influential of England's American colonists. Seeking religious freedom, the heroic Pilgrims set sail for distant shores. En route to America, these poor, pure-hearted souls invented democracy with the famed Mayflower Compact. After struggling through the initial hardships of life on unfamiliar soil, they invented the classic American holiday of Thanksgiving, which they celebrated with their friends the Indians. More virtuous than the rapacious Virginians who preceded them, the Pilgrims were the first true Americans.

Those inspiring Pilgrims of my youth have taken a beating! According to today's historians, the Pilgrims were among the least significant of England's American colonists. Their tiny Plymouth Colony was soon absorbed by the larger and more-prosperous Massachusetts Bay. The Pilgrims were no friendlier to Indians than other Europeans in the Americas—which is to say, they were greedy, duplicitous purveyors of genocide. Nor did they invent democracy: the Mayflower Compact was just an expedient means of maintaining order in a new environment. And their first "Thanksgiving" was nothing more than a replica of a traditional, secular English harvest feast. The Pilgrims didn't even call themselves Pilgrims, a term coined by the nineteenth-century Americans who invented these virtuous forbears out of thin air in an effort to grace the relatively new United States with a glorious past. Indeed, about the only aspect of my schoolboy Pilgrims that has survived this assault is their poverty.

The truth about the Pilgrims—and, yes, I do still call them Pilgrims—is perhaps closer to the "myth" than to what we can learn from today's textbooks. The vast gulf between what I once learned and what is now taught to schoolchildren is revealed in two recent books from the National Geographic Society, *1621: A New Look at Thanksgiving* and *Mayflower 1620: A New Look at a Pilgrim Voyage*, both of which recite a litany of inaccuracies as representing the fruits of "careful research of primary sources."[1] Yet, in fact, they derive their information from identifiable secondary sources of dubious alloy in order to strip the Pilgrims of the characteristics that once made them appear so unique. These books describe the settlers of Plymouth Colony as people who were united only in their "desire to own land and provide a good future for their children."

Repeatedly we are told they "didn't even call themselves Pilgrims." This can be traced to James Deetz and Patricia Scott Deetz, whose book *The Times of Their Lives: Life, Love, and Death in Plymouth Colony* (2000), maintains that "the people of Plymouth never perceived themselves as a group that would . . . come to be known as Pilgrims" and that they "were not referred to as 'Pilgrims' until the end of the 18th century." The Deetzes are repeating the opinions of George F. Willison, whose book *Saints and Strangers* (1945) claims that the "Pilgrims had no name for themselves as a group." For Willison, "in the history and saga of the Pilgrims . . . nothing is more curious than this—that their very name, 'the Pilgrims,' is little more than a century old, having come into common usage since 1840," when it began "to make its way into print."

Willison is quite wrong. He overlooks the founding of the Pilgrim Society in 1820 with its museum Pilgrim Hall and the use of the name in poems, histories, and school books from the 1790s through the 1830s, besides the publication of William Bradford's now famous phrase in Nathaniel Morton's *New England's Memorial*, first issued in 1669, and republished in 1721, 1772, and twice in 1826: "they knew that they were pilgrims and strangers here below." The Pilgrims first used that reference (cf. Hebrews 11:13–16) in print in 1622. There is absolutely no doubt that they did consider themselves "strangers and pilgrims." It is simply misleading to suggest otherwise.

Echoing the Deetzes, *1621: A New Look at Thanksgiving* states that "the 1621 gathering in Plymouth was not a religious gathering but most likely a harvest celebration much like those the English had known in farming communities back home. The English never once used the word 'thanksgiving' in association with their 1621 harvest celebration." Yet Edward Winslow's 1622 account of the feast is filled with biblical allusions his audience surely understood. When he wrote that "our Governor sent foure men on fowling; so that we might after a more speciall manner rejoyce together, after we had gathered the fruit of our labours," his readers could recognize references to John 4:36

and Psalm 33. The first is "And he that reapeth receiueth wages, & gathereth frute unto life eternal, that bothe he that soweth, & he yt [that] reapeth, might reioyce together." The second says, "Reioyce in the Lord, o ye righteous: for it becometh vpright men to be thankefull. . . . Beholde, the eye of the Lord is vpon them that feare him, & vpon them, that trust in his mercie, To deliver their soules from death, and to preserve them in famine. . . . Surely our heart shal reioyce in him, because we trusted in his holie Name." Moreover, the idea that there was some irreligious, secular folk background in England is erroneous. Although the Pilgrims preferred extemporaneous prayers, "A Thanksgiving for Plenty" (from *The* [Anglican Church's] *Book of Common Prayer*) is really, literally what "the English had known in farming communities back home," repeating the words year after year in celebrations where, by the combined authority of state and church, a harvest home simply was not what the Deetzes call a "secular event."

Mayflower 1620 introduces a new misinterpretation of the Mayflower Compact, one that is astonishing because it is so easily contradicted by the document itself. The book claims that the Compact "emphasized 'submission and obedience' to God, the English king, and the company of merchant investors that had granted the colonists permission to settle in English territory." Nineteenth-century historians who thought the document represented the beginnings of democracy in New England were mistaken. In fact, however, the text of the Mayflower Compact nowhere mentions the merchant investors, and the term *submission and obedience* is clearly used in a pledge not to God and the king but to the "civill body politic" and its "just and equal laws, ordinances, acts, constitutions, [and] offices" established by this covenant entered into mutually "in the presence of God and one of another." Moreover, regardless of further influence, it must be admitted that Plymouth Colony was the first sustained English settlement in New England and that incontrovertibly the Mayflower Compact did establish its democratic government by the mutual consent of the colony's free men.

Willison's Pilgrims were "simple and humble folk of plebeian origin, [who] read no earthshaking import into what they were doing." Their colony was riven by conflict between religious fanatics, or "Saints," from the Leiden Separatist congregation, and the group Willison calls "Strangers," whom he characterizes as unreflective members of the Church of England. As for the Mayflower Compact, "it was conceived as an instrument to maintain the *status quo* on the *Mayflower*, to show inferiors in general and servants in particular their place and keep them there where they belonged—i.e., under the thumbs of their masters." *Mayflower 1620* retains Willison's conception of the Compact as an instrument subjecting the majority of the colonists to the authority of a minority.

Samuel Eliot Morison remarked that, "the contention of a recent writer, George F. Willison, that the Pilgrim story (or 'saga' as he calls it) 'was wholly the creation of the 19th century,' is nonsense." Morison, nonetheless, accepted Willison's assumptions about the genesis of the Mayflower Compact and claiming to speak for "the unpleasant tribe of professional historians" denied that the document was more than a temporary expedient solution to the problem of governance on board the *Mayflower*. Continuing that view, it is frequently thought that the Pilgrims themselves were happy enough, even relieved, to supplant the Compact with the Second Pierce Patent (1621) and, eventually, the Bradford (or Warwick) Patent of 1629–30. The "unpleasant tribe" thus interprets the Mayflower Compact as a document with very limited real significance when drawn up but subsequently of great symbolic use after its promotion in 1802 by John Quincy Adams as a major milestone in the creation of American identity.

As agreed in the Compact, equal members of the community would establish and abide by their own bylaws and ordinances, by which they would choose their own officers from among themselves. If this were a temporary expedient, one would expect the Pilgrims to forget the Mayflower Compact and rejoice in its being superseded by the two later patents. The text was first published in 1622 in the booklet now known as *Mourt's Relation*, indicating that in the earliest years the Mayflower Compact was regarded as a document worthy of public attention. Later court records show that the Compact was far from forgotten. At three important points, the colonists cite the Compact as their constitution and the later charters as augmentations. In the "Form to be placed before the Records of the Several Inheritances granted to all and every the King's subjects inhabiting within the Government of New Plymouth" (1633), we read that the colonists "entered into a Civill combinacion being the eleventh of November [1620] as the subjects of our said Sov. Lord the King to become a Body-politick binding ourselves to observe such lawes & ordinances and obey such Officers as from time to time should be made & chosen for our wel ordering & guideance. And thereupon by the favor of the Almighty began the first Colony in New England." The Pierce and Bradford patents are then named as enlargements. The same formulation precedes the codification of the colony laws in the 1658 "Declaration demonstrating the warrantable grounds and proceedings of the first Associates of the Government of New Plymouth in theire laying the first foundation of the Government in this jurisdiction for the making of Lawes." It recurs identically in the preface to the *Book of the General Laws . . . of New Plymouth*, published in Boston in New England in 1685.

Emphatically, the Mayflower Compact remained the foundation and formative constitution of Plymouth Colony. Put to paper in circumstances of potential division, it was a well-grounded composition, rooted in Dissenting —Congregationalist—theology, which ensured a future of democratic government by elected officials and magistrates following laws proposed and accepted by the people and their representatives. It was not an ad hoc expedient replaced soon after by another piece of paper and quickly forgotten until rediscovered by John Quincy Adams.

Mayflower 1620 tells schoolchildren that the Pilgrims "dug up stores of buried corn, as well as Wampanoag graves. Few of the colonists considered this stealing. Most of them had little or no respect for those they called Indians or savages." No evidence justifies the statement "few of the colonists considered," and the only evidence we have regarding graves consists of Winslow's statements explicitly contradicting *Mayflower 1620*. Pilgrim explorers discovered "a bow with rotted arrows" in a mound they investigated: "We supposed there were many other things, but because we deemed them graves, we put in the bow again and made it up as it was, and left the rest untouched, because we thought it would be odious unto them to ransack their sepulchres."

The National Geographic Society's *1621: A New Look at Thanksgiving* instructs schoolchildren that "much of what was written at the time about Native people is wrong or distorted." This belief reflects the opinions of Francis Jennings's book *The Invasion of America, Indians, Colonialism, and the Cant of Conquest* (1975). Jennings considers colonial leaders self-serving liars whose word should never be taken at face value. Jennings infers outrageous deceptive intent from the fact that recorded agreements between Indians and colonists no longer exist. He is sure that to protect their own future reputations, the colonists destroyed evidence of underhanded dealings with the people whose land they robbed and whose culture they suppressed. Jennings takes no notice of the fire on December 21, 1747, in which, according to an eyewitness, the colony secretary, "All the Books of the General Court, Governor & Council & House of Representatives there in the House were wholly lost without saving one & all the Books of Commissions and other Instruments as well from the Crown as the Government of the Province with most of ye original papers are likewise consumed." Jennings's conspiratorial version of colonial history is widely accepted, despite being contradicted by all primary evidence (but the evidence, he claims, is wrong or distorted). Probably this attitude underlies the plaintive wish for an arcane oral history that could tell us the way natives experienced the events—a desire so strong it has inspired much obvious invention of the "they would've thought" sort. Perhaps we can discover in this attitude the rationale in these National Geographic books for replacing Edward Winslow's careful descriptions of native culture with the vague musings of the late Nanepashemet (Anthony Pollard), who, growing up in New Bedford in the 1970s, became interested in Wampanoags, read everything available to him on the subject, left school, changed his name, and gradually achieved oracular status through inspiringly grand pronouncements, such as "We have lived with this land for thousands of generations." No admission that stories might be modified in retelling inhibits the notion that "the oral histories of the Wampanoag people—the spoken words that have been passed on from generation to generation for thousands of years—have continued into the present."

The book *1621: A New Look at Thanksgiving* abounds with tendentious generalizations, such as "It was not unusual for Europeans to kidnap Native people as curiosities." But in New England this *was* unusual. Winslow was not alone in protesting the unacceptable inhumanity displayed by two English captains whose kidnaping of coastal Indians had poisoned relations with the natives for the Pilgrims who came a few years later. "The colonists thought they had a right to help themselves to whatever they pleased," we learn. Never mind that Winslow details the efforts, ultimately successful after several months, to locate and pay native owners of corn removed from storage baskets—to provide compensation for what must have looked like theft. The National Geographic book ignores the Pilgrims' belief that their settlement at Plymouth was confirmed "by a peaceable composition" [or land grant] from Massasoit Osamequen. Winslow, like Roger Williams, firmly acknowledged native title to land. Native land tenure in the area of Plymouth Colony during the seventeenth century was, however, personal and hereditary, not these books' neo-Romantic notion of tribal land "owned by none, but held and used with respect by all."

Both National Geographic books were created in collaboration with Plimoth Plantation Museum—their stated intention being to represent "new thinking." "Unquestioning acceptance of biased interpretations can affect the way we treat one another, even today," we are told in the foreword to one of them. Despite these pious sentiments, the museum's participation was not sufficient to save the authors (admittedly not historians) from replacing shopworn straw-man stereotypes with nothing more than a new-mixed potion of politically correct invention.

The theme of Plymouth Colony's isolation and insignificance was initiated by Arthur Percival Norton in 1914, elaborated by Willison in 1945, and repeated by A. L. Rowse, who wrote in 1959 that the Pilgrims' importance has been greatly exaggerated. For Morison, Plymouth's colonists were simple people but courageous. Darrett B. Rutman, in 1967, considered Plymouth Colony "a backwater, its people quiet and basically conservative, seldom rising above the ordinary round of daily work." Rutman's conclusions are cited by the Deetzes to justify emphasizing "stasis rather than change." Their colonists lived "largely uneventful lives, dictated by the change of seasons, year after year." What made them interesting was neither idealism nor religious or political innovation—no great thoughts or deeds—but the details of ordinary lives of superstition, fornication, drunkenness, violent crime, and primitive housing.

This undisturbed isolation is contradicted by a crisis that occurred in 1645, when the majority of Plymouth Colony's magistrates were prepared to support a motion for complete and unrestricted religious liberty. Only prejudice or unfamiliarity with the historical record explains overlooking this remarkable ripple in axiomatically stagnant waters. Were the governments of England and The Netherlands looking for a backwater simpleton when they appointed Edward Winslow to chair an international committee to resolve their countries' differences in 1654? Was it uneventful that objections to persecution of Quakers in New England, coauthored by the colony magistrate James Cudworth, were published in London in 1659 under the title *The Secret Workes of a Cruel People Made Manifest?*

Ironically, the only point of agreement between the old and new myths is refuted by the documentary evidence. The Pilgrims were neither isolated nor poor. By the second half of the seventeenth century, Scituate was the largest and, in economic terms, the most important town in Plymouth Colony. Sixteen levies between 1666 and 1686 rate Scituate consistently about 60 percent higher than the assessment for the town of Plymouth. Similar sources confirm the pattern, yet Scituate is given no prominence in histories of Plymouth Colony and is entirely overlooked in further studies, such as Bernard Bailyn's *New England Merchants in the Seventeenth Century* (1955). Scituate is not even on the map of "Southern New England in the early 1670s" illustrating Alden T. Vaughan's *New England Frontier: Puritans and Indians, 1620–1675* (1965). Morison found "very little evidence of people in Plymouth colony owning ships or building anything bigger than a small sloop." Similarly George D. Langdon said, "Few, if any, men with commercial contact in England seem to have settled in Plymouth Colony until after the opening of the Mount Hope lands in the 1680s" and that "the absence of mercantile contacts in England and the limits imposed by geography prevented the establishment of a trans-atlantic commerce." Both Morison and Langdon were familiar with—but brushed aside—the mercantile activities of Isaac Allerton, who traveled repeatedly back and forth to England and whose expanding commercial interests are recorded in Plymouth Colony, Massachusetts Bay, New Haven, New Netherland, Newfoundland, New Sweden, Virginia, Barbados, and Curaçao. Both had read Bradford, who records the names of five ships (besides the *Mayflower*) owned or used by the Pilgrims for transatlantic commerce in the 1620s and 1630s and notes numerous visits to Plymouth harbor by Dutch and English merchantmen. Governor John Winthrop of Massachusetts Bay recorded that in the 1630s, Plymouth colonists had much trade with the Dutch at Hudson's River. Neither Morison nor Langdon, however, used the very extensive town records of Scituate, where early references to shipbuilding are found. Neither paid attention to the commerce of colony residents Miles Standish, Edward Winslow, Thomas Willett, Timothy Hatherley, William Vassall, Thomas Tart, Peter and Anthony Collamore, and John Cushing, who engaged in trade with England, New Netherland, and the West Indies. Instead of cosmopolitan colonial trade, we read about isolated pioneers bickering along in congealed social antagonisms, who managed somehow to achieve a degree of backwoods heroism, or, alternatively, to impose their crude, insensitive ways on a superior society first weakened by imported disease.

We all think we know about Plymouth Colony and the Pilgrims, but have we been getting it wrong—again and again? Does political fashion require that we exchange old bunk for new?

NOTE

1. Catherine O'Neill Grace and Margaret M. Bruchac, with Plimoth Plantation, photographs by Sisse Brimberg and Cotton Coulson, *1621: A New Look at Thanksgiving* (Washington, D.C.: National Geographic Society, 2001); Plimoth Plantation with Peter Arenstam, John Kemp, and Catherine O'Neill Grace, photographs by Sisse Brimberg and Cotton Coulson, *Mayflower 1620: A New Look at a Pilgrim Voyage* (Washington, D.C.: National Geographic Society, 2003).

What Happened to the Puritans?

Thomas S. Kidd

"What happened to the Puritans?" Among American historians, the classic answer to that question is that their religious commitment declined, and they became Yankees.[1] In doing so they became quintessential Americans, moralizing and acquisitive at the same time. Historians of colonial New England have long recognized problems with this story, however. First, we don't know when to mark the end of Puritanism. The era between the Salem witchcraft trials (1692) and the Great Awakening (1740s) is a veritable "dark ages" of historical understanding. We reflexively call New Englanders "Puritans" through 1740, while knowing that the label can't possibly fit any more. Second, the "declension" narrative doesn't account for the remarkable persistence of religious identity among these no-longer Puritans. We keep expecting the Puritans, like Americans, to stop being so religious. Though religion changes, however, it doesn't seem to go away. It is time to reevaluate the end of Puritanism. New Englanders' public religion changed after Puritanism, but it did not decline. Instead, after 1689, many New Englanders became profoundly attached to a movement they called the "Protestant interest," the faithful community of world Protestants fighting against world Catholics. While the Puritans of the seventeenth century, fleeing authorities in England, had been inwardly focused, the Protestant interest looked to the British nation as the last great hope for Protestants to defeat the Catholic menace. They hoped that the defeat of global Catholicism might herald the return of Christ.

Any attempt precisely to mark the end of Puritanism as a movement would, of course, represent an imposition for narrative's convenience. Movements like Puritanism don't "end" in one moment. However, we can surely say that once the Glorious Revolution was embraced by New Englanders, their religious and political agenda had so fundamentally changed that it doesn't make sense to call them Puritans any longer. The rise of the Protestant interest explains a great deal about how prominent New Englanders responded to the massive changes they faced in the decades after 1689.

New Englanders grew heavily invested in the military and imperial successes of the British nation after the Glorious Revolution, when Britain became embroiled in almost a century of war with Catholic France and/or Spain. New Englanders were deeply implicated in these wars and feared that the depredations suffered by French Protestants after the Revocation of the Edict of Nantes (1685) would visit them, too. Their position south of Quebec made them, if anything, more vulnerable to French attacks than their fellow countrypeople in Britain. Many New Englanders paid close attention to the fate of Protestants in Europe. They noted with considerable concern the growing violence between Catholics and Protestants in far-off places like the Palatinate and Poland. Pastors encouraged their congregations to pray for the persecuted Protestants of Europe and warned them that the divine judgment of Catholic invasion could easily come against them next, should they fail in their holy responsibilities to family, church, and state. The Glorious Revolution, the wars with Catholic powers, and a deepening sense of common cause with international Protestantism led New Englanders to shed many vestiges of their old Puritan identity in favor of a new identification with the Protestant interest.

In the seventeenth century, the Puritans struggled ever to make common cause with other Protestants because of squabbles over doctrine and church polity. Moreover, Massachusetts and Connecticut had been founded because of their leaders' hostility to the English church and state. New Englanders famously fled England because of persecution in the 1620s and 1630s. Oliver Cromwell's regime had offered false hope that the Puritans would establish a godly government in England, and the Restoration in 1660 shattered the Puritans' dreams of reforming English church and state. The direction of the monarchy only became more horrifying as Charles II secretly and James II openly embraced Catholicism. Another reason that New Englanders despised James II so much was because he had revoked Massachusetts's charter in the 1680s and placed it and the other New England colonies under the new Dominion of New England. Once William and Mary took the throne in 1688, many hoped that Massachusetts would get its old charter back, securing its basic freedoms from British meddling. There was much initial controversy over the new Massachusetts charter of 1692 because it gave much more authority over the province to the British government and because it required the former Puritans to tolerate all Protestants, even Anglicans. Yet leaders in Massachusetts soon became quite willing to shoulder their role in the British nation.

Indeed, the most remarkable difference between Puritanism and the Protestant interest concerned the dominant opinion of the British nation. Now, abandoning their seventeenth-century precisionism, New Englanders became intensely devoted to the British nation, empire, and monarchy, especially as Britain fought perceived Catholic enemies within and outside its borders. They came to see the new British government as the leader in the fight against world Catholicism and thought it foolhardy to undermine the power of the monarchy or the empire in the name of intra-Protestant squabbles.

Leading pastors in New England, especially Boston's Benjamin Colman, now expressed undying loyalty to Britain and the Protestant succession in numerous public proclamations. Colman, the most internationally influential pastor in New England in the decades before the Great Awakening of the 1740s, was the model advocate for the Protestant interest. In a host of public sermons and addresses, he insisted on New Englanders' devotion to the British nation and international Protestantism. The height of his rhetoric of British nationalism came in 1727 when he equated support for the new king, George II, with attachment to the cause of Christ. In *Fidelity to Christ and to the Protestant Succession in the Illustrious House of Hannover,* Colman framed the succession of George II as the next step in the providential history of the monarchy beginning with William in 1688. Colman stated baldly that "Our faithful zeal for and adherence to the Protestant Succession in the House of Hannover, is our fidelity to CHRIST and his holy Religion."

Colman also regularly excoriated fellow countrypeople who appeared disloyal to British Protestantism, especially the Jacobites, who sought a return of the Stuart heir to the throne. New Englanders knew that their loyalty to the Protestant succession was useful politically, as most Britons could agree that Jacobites were despicable traitors. Thus, though there seems to have been almost no Jacobites in New England, the leaders there constantly denounced Jacobitism and reminded the monarch that Jacobitism had no friends in New England. Some Anglican authorities in Britain looked askance at New England's dissenting establishment, but as long as the focus remained on maintaining the Protestant succession, there was no place for intra-Protestant feuding. After the death of Queen Anne in 1714, New Englanders had great confidence that they could make common cause with low-church Anglicans in a British Protestant cohort.

Print media also helped create the new identification with the Protestant interest. The newspapers, especially the *Boston News-Letter* (founded 1704), maintained a remarkable commitment in their early decades to supplying news of persecuted and warring Protestants in Europe. Confessing his fondness for such international news, Jonathan Edwards remembered, "I had great longings for the advancement of Christ's kingdom in the world.... If I heard the least hint of anything that happened in any part of the world, that appeared to me, in some respect or other, to have a favorable aspect on the interest of Christ's kingdom, my soul eagerly catched at it.... I used to be earnest to read public news-letters, mainly for that end; to see if I could not find some news favorable to the interest of religion in the world." Many pastors used such available knowledge to call for prayer for the suffering Protestant churches and to help New Englanders identify vitally with their distant brethren.

The popular New England almanacs also helped serve the interests of British Protestantism, especially through the admiration they expressed for the monarchs and the way they reminded readers of key moments in British providential history. The almanacs' calendars, which almost never acknowledged holidays like Christmas, did list important dates in the history of the Protestant monarchy. No other notable day appeared with more regularity on the almanacs' calendars than the Gunpowder Plot, November 5. This date became doubly important in the memory of British Protestantism because it marked the foiling of the Catholic Guy Fawkes's attempt to blow up Parliament in 1605 as well as King William's invasion in 1688 to oust the Catholic King James II. In New England, where almanac makers and many of their readers felt uncomfortable with any holidays associated with the Anglican church calendar, November 5 seemed a holiday that nearly everyone could enjoy, for it signified defeats for Catholicism.

The danger posed by Catholicism became most immediate to New Englanders in times of war, especially during the largely forgotten Father Rale's War of 1722–25. This war manifested all the fears New Englanders entertained about the Catholic enemy. They had heard for years about the threat posed by world Catholicism to the international Protestant movement, and in the 1720s, they faced attacks from northeastern Wabanakis encouraged by Sebastien Rale, the French Jesuit missionary in Norridgewock, Maine. Though Rale seemed driven by a desire to protect the Wabanakis' land rights, New Englanders thought the war represented a satanic attempt to destroy their outpost of Protestantism in North America. In 1724 Massachusetts sent a war party to Norridgewock, where they executed and scalped Rale and many of his mission Indians. Boston pastor Cotton Mather rejoiced, writing that "the Barbarous and Perfidous Indians in our Eastern Country, being Moved by the Instigation of the Devil and Father Rallee; have begun Hostilities upon us. They did it, when the French Hopes of a Fatal Revolution on the British Empire, deceived them. And it was not long before the Hairy Scalp of that Head in the House of the Wicked, paid for what Hand he had in the Rebellion." The war was not motivated by legitimate grievances, according to Mather, but by "the Devil and Father Rallee." Rale paid for it with his scalp and life.

Finally, leaders of the Protestant interest lived in a mental world filled with eschatological expectations that fueled their intense anti-Catholicism and loyalty both to Britain and the international Protestant community. Many expected that before Christ's return, the Catholic Church would be destroyed, the Jewish people would be converted to Christianity, and the once-threatened Protestant churches would lead miraculous revivals. New Englanders sought to insert themselves into these apocalyptic dramas by fighting against the Catholic threat, praying for the conversion of the Jews and other non-Christians, and ultimately, by promoting their own revivals. Boston's John Webb in 1734 begged his people to pray for revival, believing that if "we can once prevail with the Lord, to Revive his Work, in these declining Years; Oh! What an happy Prospect shall we have!" Then, he argued, would come the fulfillment of one of the most frequently referenced Old Testament prophecies among the Protestant interest, Isaiah 44:3–5: "I will pour water upon him that is thirsty, and floods upon the dry ground: I will pour out my spirit upon thy Seed, and my Blessing upon thine Offspring. . . . One shall say, I am the Lord's: and another shall subscribe unto the Lord, and sirname himself by the name of Israel." To the friends of the Protestant interest, the time had come for the reformed Christians of the British Atlantic world to come before God and plead for the great end-time revival and for a great eschatological turn in which millions would repent and "sirname" themselves as the millennial people of God. To many, the great outpouring of the Holy Spirit for revival seemed finally to come with the arrival of the young Anglican itinerant, George Whitefield.

It is of great importance, then, that the Protestant interest may not just help explain the end of Puritanism but also the rise of evangelicalism. The Protestant interest's fascination with the global fate of Protestantism fed directly into the hope that revivals could turn the world to Christ and Protestantism. In 1740 Boston's Thomas Prince preached a remarkable sermon on Protestant internationalism and evangelical expansion, *The Endless Increase of Christ's Government*. In it, he envisioned the eschatological triumph of the gospel: "For as this gospel of the kingdom shall be preached in all the world, for a witness to all nations, before the end of this present state shall come . . . I cannot expect, that not only all the southern, western, and north-western parts of this new world, and Calefornia, will, in their times, be full of pure and pious churches, rejoicing in the great Redeemer; but even all that further western continent, extending from America to Asia, and that the gospel will go round and conquer every nation in Japan and China, Tartary, India, Persia, Africa, and Egypt, until it return to Zion, where it rose." The Protestant interest's belief in the deep cultural crisis of Protestantism and the coming revivals of the last days helped create the new evangelical movement, too.

We must be careful to note that many associated with the Protestant interest did not become evangelicals. The core beliefs of the Protestant interest—anti-Catholicism, British nationalism, and Protestant internationalism—were more widely shared than sympathy for the revivals of the 1740s would be. Nevertheless, many leaders of the Protestant interest did also become evangelicals, including Benjamin Colman. It was Colman, after all, who received news in 1735 that Jonathan Edwards had begun to see great new concern for religion in his church. Colman requested from Edwards a "Particular account of the Present Extraordinary circumstances . . . with Respect to Religion" in western New England. When Edwards responded to Colman with an eight-page narrative of the revival that soon became *A Faithful Narrative of the Surprising Work of God,* a chain of events was set into motion that would eventually help generate the massive awakenings in New England, the Middle Colonies, and Britain in the 1740s.

The concept of the Protestant interest provides a whole new framework for how to tell the story of colonial New England. It is surprising that it has taken us this long to do so, since New England has received the preponderance of historians' attention in colonial America. The Protestant interest lifts the middle decades of colonial New England's history out of its traditional muddle. Puritanism did not linger on as a shell of its former self after 1689. New England's civil religion did not decline in the decades before the 1740s; it changed. Similarly evangelicalism did not emerge out of worn-out and guilty Puritanism. The revivals of the 1740s may no longer be "surprising," as Jonathan Edwards put it. The Protestant interest was the missing link between Puritanism and evangelicalism.

NOTE

1. The best-known accounts of New England's "declension" are Perry Miller, *The New England Mind: From Colony to Province* (Cambridge, Mass.: Harvard University Press, 1953), and Richard Bushman, *From Puritan to Yankee: Character and the Social Order in Connecticut, 1690–1765* (Cambridge, Mass.: Harvard University Press, 1967).

The Great Meadow

Sustainable Husbandry in Colonial Concord

Brian Donahue

History has not been kind to New England farmers.[1] Colonial husbandmen have long been cast as crude, extensive farmers: because land was plentiful and labor scarce, it is alleged, they depleted soil fertility and cleared new land rather than caring intensively for what they already had in cultivation. Beginning with the anonymous (and non-American) author of *American Husbandry* in 1775, gentlemen routinely accused these yeomen of mistreating livestock and wasting manure. Nineteenth-century agricultural improvers condemned the plodding ways of their own forefathers. They followed the lead of Yale president Timothy Dwight, who famously wrote that "the principal defects in our husbandry, so far as I am able to judge, are a deficiency in the quantity of labor necessary to prepare the ground for seed, insufficient manuring, the want of a good rotation of crops, and slovenliness in cleaning the ground."[2]

Modern historians have mostly agreed. But interestingly, they have offered two diametrically opposed explanations for this slovenliness. Some claim that subsistence farmers lacked market incentives to improve. Others argue that the market imperative to commodify nature encouraged them to degrade the land. The first, neoclassical view was crystallized by Percy Bidwell in 1921 and has prevailed among economic historians to this day. Like Dwight, these scholars attribute inefficient use of land and labor to structural barriers. Once markets emerged in the second quarter of the nineteenth century (said Bidwell—Winifred Rothenberg pushed the transition back to the last quarter of the eighteenth century), New England agriculture began to show signs of improvement but then, by the same remorseless logic, sank beneath competition from farms on better soils to the west.[3]

Environmental historians, notably William Cronon and Carolyn Merchant, have proposed another explanation for exhaustive farming in colonial New England that runs counter to the progressive idea that greater market penetration led to improved use of land. In their view, the English colonists turned a native land of ecological harmony based on usufruct into a privatized "world of fields and fences." They have argued that the expanding market economy of the colonial Atlantic world drove the newcomers to commodify and exploit natural resources as rapidly as possible, rather than conserve them as the Indians had done—clearing forest, depleting wildlife, exhausting soils, eroding hillsides, fouling streams. Cronon had this occurring from the moment the English landed; Merchant had the exploitation worsening with the market revolution of the early nineteenth century. In any event, the degradation of land that was once seen as the mark of isolated subsistence farming is ascribed precisely to the market itself.[4]

All of these historians have accepted that colonial New England husbandry was extensive and ultimately exhausting, although they fit that description into very different interpretive frameworks. But how do we know that colonial husbandry was like that—beyond taking Timothy Dwight and Arthur Young at their word? The answer, as far as I can tell, is that we don't know it was like that. There isn't much evidence for it. In fact, it's hard to imagine how early New England towns like Concord could actually have been farmed extensively for the entire colonial period.

The landscape of Concord certainly was degraded by 1850. Forest had been driven to a low of 11 percent, and increased river flooding was spoiling hay meadows. Run-down, unproductive pastures were growing up in brush. Henry David Thoreau and George Perkins Marsh, the Yankee grandsires of the conservation movement, had it right: the nineteenth-century boom in agricultural clearing in New England came at the expense of the land.[5] But was this the consequence of two centuries of deeply ingrained bad habits that had not been sufficiently improved upon? Or was it because of a more recent transformation, the early nineteenth-century market revolution? To find out how New England farming took shape, I mapped seventeenth-century land divisions in Concord (thirty thousand acres divided into more than eight hundred very odd little pieces) and the ownership and use of a few thousand of those acres from 1635 to present, using deeds, probated estates, tax valuations, and GIS (geographic information system) software. What follows is a summary of my findings concerning the colonial period and my corollary proposition concerning the early nineteenth century.

The Great Meadow

In 1792 recent Harvard graduate William Jones wrote of his native town "the soil is various; consisting of rocky, sandy, and moist land; but it is in general fertile." This division of soils into three distinct types had shaped the way Concord farmers worked the land for six generations. Rocky land comprised uplands formed of glacial till, deposited directly beneath the retreating glacial ice. It was cold, stony, and hard to plow, but the underlying hard pan held water and made it good for pastures and orchards. Sandy land was formed by outwash into melt-water streams and lakes and was warm and workable, though dry. Some coarse soils were too droughty to cultivate, but the finer sandy loams made decent tillage. Moist land included silt dropped at the bottom of glacial lakes, along with more-recent alluvial deposits. These mucks and peats were rich in organic matter but low-lying and wet. Not all Concord soils were full of big rocks—they were marginal in many *different* ways. But while they may not have had the intrinsic fertility of prairie soils, taken together they presented a full complement of useful capabilities to the enterprising husbandman.[6]

The town of Concord was founded in 1635, the first inland plantation to be settled in Massachusetts Bay colony. The native people living there had fashioned ways of working with the diverse soils, vegetation, and wildlife of Musketaquid (as they called it) that had endured for thousands of years. But there may be more than one way to sustainably inhabit the same place. The English yeomen who displaced the natives had spent many generations developing a complex mixed-husbandry system in their own homeland. How did they go about adapting that system to New England, and how well did it stand up over time? The English arrived as their world was undergoing a capitalist transformation, so a parallel question might be: Does the pattern by which land was settled and farmed in Concord indicate a system of diverse local production and exchange expanding through demographic growth or a system driven primarily by commercial production for outside markets?

The English were drawn to Concord by abandoned planting fields but above all by an abundance of native hay along the river. In this "wildernesse" they set down a classic English open-field village, hard by the Great Meadow. By 1653 about fifty house lots were tightly clustered within a mile of the meetinghouse and millpond. Surrounding the house lots were several arable fields, including the Great Field, two miles long and a mile wide. Meadow lots were strung along every waterway, from the Mill Brook flowing through the village and the Great Meadow just downstream to remote meadows in every corner of town. The remaining three-quarters of the town served as commons upon which to graze livestock and cut wood and timber. The colonists had adopted several native plants (maize, pumpkins, beans, and meadow hay grasses) but had put in place a system of husbandry that relied on as many English elements (rye, apples, sod-forming pasture grasses, cattle, hogs, sheep) and a thoroughly English ecological structure.

We can get an idea of how the system was organized by looking at the First Division holdings of William Hartwell, a middling man who hailed from Bedfordshire. By 1653 Hartwell owned eighty-six acres in fourteen widely scattered pieces. Hartwell's plow land was located a half mile from his door in the Great Field, a mile away in the Brick Kiln Field, and even two miles distant in the Chestnut Field (although that "field" may actually have been growing chestnuts). The great problem presented by this traditional open-field pattern was how to deliver manure to such widely dispersed tillage lots. In England, this had been accomplished by summer folding of livestock in front of the winter crop and by mucking the spring crop with barnyard manure. But in Concord the spring grain (maize) demanded almost all the dung, whereas the winter grain (rye) got almost none. Added to that, New England offered scant winter grazing but instead livestock was fed at home for almost six months with stored fodder. This meant that much more of the year's dung accumulated in the yard and had to be carted out at planting time. In Concord, open field rotations and far-flung tillage lots were a liability. As the town was fully settled, most general fields dissolved, and tracts of good plow land gathered small neighborhood clusters of homesteads about them. The object, I believe, was to get the barns close to the cornfields for ease of mucking. These home fields were then cultivated year after year, generation after generation.

Hartwell also owned eight mowing lots: in Bridge Meadow before his house, in the Great Meadow, in Elm Brook Meadow, and in distant Rocky Meadow three miles away. These meadows provided hay to bring the cattle through the winter and thus also provided manure to the tilled fields. They were the foundation of this system of husbandry. Because of the long winters, Concord settlers required two or three times more hay than they had in England. They immediately granted themselves far-flung mowing lots in all the wet places they could find, no matter how remote. This wide scattering among diverse river and brook meadows persisted unchanged into the nineteenth century.

Finally, like his neighbors, Hartwell had access to the three-quarters of the town that remained as commons for grazing and wood. However, like many other early New England towns, Concord moved away from the commons system after the first generation. Most of the remaining land was privatized in a great "Second Division" that began in 1653 and took several decades to complete. When all the land was divided, Hartwell had become the owner of twenty pieces of land amounting to 250 acres. Most of Concord's aging proprietors received their grants in this irregular way. They were acquiring equitable (though not equal) proportions of a diverse array of necessary resources and endowing land banks to provide legacies for their numerous sons and grandsons.

Settling this land was a slow, orderly process. It took three or four generations to cover the three or four miles to the borders of Concord. Meanwhile, the unsettled outlands often continued to provide grazing for the common herd. One son (frequently the youngest) carried on the original village holding while others moved to the outskirts and still others to new towns on the frontier, often to land that had served as backcountry pasture while being cleared. Hartwell's youngest son, Samuel, inherited the homeplace, while elder son, John, squeezed in next door. Not until the 1690s would William's meadow and upland at Rocky Meadow provide the core of a new farm for his grandson Samuel. There appears to have been no contradiction between the maintenance of a stable ecological and social order within Concord and the dynamic movement to new lands and new towns. Neither the decline of community nor the depletion of old land was a driving force, as far as I can see—just big families and a strong desire to colonize land and replicate the system across New England. The *pull* of available land may have brought forth large families as much as the *push* of "too many" children necessitated migration.

The Meriam family, who lived about a half mile east of the Hartwells on the edge of the village, illustrates this process. Meriam's corner was settled by John Meriam of the second generation in the 1660s. By 1710 John had split the homeland among three of his sons while two others had moved to his Second Division outlands two miles away in what later became the town of Bedford. Ebenezer Meriam inherited the old house, while John Jr. and Joseph built new houses close by, within a shout: the *houses* were consolidated while the *land* was scrambled. At the height of their careers, in 1735, these three brothers worked forty parcels of land, scattered up to three miles away. By the fourth generation in 1749, this pattern had intensified still further. Now there were four Meriam households, with intricately intermixed tillage and meadow lots surrounding the houses. The Meriams did this not by necessity but by choice.

Most Concord families worked land in a similarly dispersed fashion, as illustrated just down the road at the old Brickiln Field. Throughout the colonial period, they reproduced a pattern of small holdings intermixed with neighbors and kin. Besides being sociable, this clustering was economically efficient in a world where both men and women were forever exchanging work and goods with these neighbors. There were ecological reasons as well. The map of land use in 1749 shows the completed adaptation of English mixed-husbandry to a section of Concord. We see careful placement of the integrated elements of farming across a diverse landscape, designed to provide a "comfortable subsistence" from local resources.

Tillage land was clustered on sandy, well-drained soils, which were often much subdivided among neighboring homesteads. All the evidence suggests that these home fields stayed put, and I see little sign of an extensive brush fallow pattern. It would have been impossible to grow corn on the same ground for generation after generation without manuring it. Dung was avidly collected and used, not neglected. In 1672, when Edward Wright agreed to keep John Hoar's livestock, it was stipulated that the dung belonged to the ground upon which it fell, not the stock that dropped it. A century later, in 1774, a cordwainer named Jacob Walker rented horse stalls in the village, "reserving yearly the dung made in each stable."[7] All the manure in Concord was spoken for.

By the late colonial period, most of the wetlands in Concord had been transformed into hay meadows. Elaborate cooperative drainage systems were required along all the brooks to remove excess water and render the meadows accessible. In some larger meadows, this was enforced by a formal Commission of Sewers, but in most it was a matter of neighborly persuasion that left no written record, only the ditches themselves, stretching for miles. The drains were cleaned in late summer or fall, and the muck was dried and carted to the barnyard to absorb urine and dung or spread directly on the light, sandy upland fields. The meadows were inexhaustible, producing coarse hay at the low but reliable level of about one ton per acre, year in and year out, for two centuries and more. Winter flooding recaptured sediments and nutrients that were shed higher in the agricultural landscape. These nutrients were returned to the plow lands, mostly in the form of hay that had been converted to manure by the cattle. The Great Meadow and other river meadows flooded naturally every winter, but many of the brook meadows were deliberately flowed to fertilize them—an ancient English custom. Usually this was arranged amicably among neighbors, but now and then farmers had to resort to law to settle who had rights to the water.[8]

Grazing was found on sandy arable land more distant from the barn that was only occasionally broken up and sown to rye; on the rich aftermath of the meadows; and on rocky till uplands slowly emerging from forest. Maintaining these pastures would prove a challenge, but through most of the colonial period, the quantity and quality of grazing in Concord rose slowly but steadily as forest was cleared and European pasture grasses, such as bluegrass, ryegrass, and white clover, became established. Ample grassland was critical to successful husbandry, as shown by the Hartwells on the upland near Rocky Meadow. Ephraim Hartwell built a house next to his father, Samuel, during the 1730s and passed the two farms to his sons in turn, and the family worked the same land until late in the nineteenth century. Their homesteads had abundant meadows and pastures, and they kept substantial cow and beef herds. With manure plentiful, their grain yields were high. Their orchards were large and fruitful: Ephraim Hartwell pressed forty barrels of cider in 1749. Apples were well adapted to rocky till and, compared to barley, saved labor and manure. On rough and rocky land that appears too marginal for farming today, these yeomen arranged the elements of their husbandry with great care and understanding, and they prospered.

On their roughest lands, Concord yeomen owned just enough woodland to supply fuel, fencing, building timber, and other necessities of the local economy, such as charcoal for the blacksmith and oak bark for the tanner. Probated estates and store account books indicate that many farmers were also sending forest products to the ports, including ship timber, barrel staves, and hoops. By the late colonial period, the woodlands were reaching the irreducible minimum needed to house and heat the inhabitants. Although Concord was straining with young husbandmen hungry to clear land, acreage in woodland stabilized at about 30 percent of the town and declined only slightly over the next half century.

Concord had put in place a well-balanced, sustainable mixed-husbandry system, skillfully adapted to a diverse, difficult environment. These yeomen did not maximize any one crop at the expense of others but aimed instead to optimize a wide range of production and exchange at the household and community levels. The interdependence of the elements of their husbandry left them tightly bound by local limits. Yes, they marketed beef and timber, but they could not cut Concord's woodlands and expand their pastures too aggressively without going cold in the winter because importing wood was prohibitively expensive. Or anyway, they *did* not—these were people who fully expected at least one branch of their descendants to inhabit the same land for generations to come.

The most critical ecological limit in Concord was the supply of meadow hay, which capped the number of stock that could be wintered. As Concord completely filled with farms, acreage in tillage reached its historic peak in the mid-eighteenth century, and grain yields scraped bottom. It wasn't that the land was "worn out"; there just wasn't enough manure to go around. Concord had encountered the classic mixed-husbandry bind: the arable land was outrunning the grass, just as it had in fourteenth- and seventeenth-century England. As the astute Connecticut minister Jared Eliot put it, "The necessary stock of the country hath outgrown the meadows."[9] Now all but one son would have to go farm somewhere else or try something other than farming.

As Concord yeomen and goodwives chafed against the limitations of local production in the nineteenth century, they found ways to join the market revolution sweeping the country. The inhabitants began to purchase more basic necessities from sources beyond Concord. They imported wheat flour, cotton cloth, Pennsylvania coal, pine lumber, and even whale oil from the far side of the world. By 1840 these cider-drinking yeomen had become temperate, tea-totaling, calculating Yankee farmers. To take part in the market economy, Concord farmers had to increase their own commercial production. They did this mostly by concentrating on grass and cows. As more bread grain was imported, and the acreage in tillage declined, grain yields (now mostly cow corn and horse oats) rebounded because more manure could be applied. Above all, Concord farmers broke through the meadow hay barrier by planting domesticated, upland "English" hay—red-top, timothy, and clover. During the second quarter of the nineteenth century, with strong urban markets for livestock products (and for the hay itself), Concord doubled its hay production. Concord became a town of hard-driven milk farmers, a few of them thriving, many mired in debt. These were Thoreau's men of quiet desperation, speculating in herds of cattle to purchase their shoestrings.

Concord was also, by then, a town of decimated forests, flooded river meadows, and exhausted pastures growing up in huckleberries and pines. No manure returned to the upland hayfields and pastures; the nutrients flowed down and away. It appears that this occurred *because* of the market revolution, not in spite of it. There were genuine improvements—better manure handling, better stock, better seeds, better tools—but the rise in productivity was mainly driven by "skinning" the land and rendering much of it "unimproved" in just a few decades. *This* is when we really see extensive farming and worn-out land in New England. The enterprising and confident improvers who led this transformation had a powerful vested interest in disowning the pinched, straitened, supposedly exhausting traditions of their forefathers. Agricultural experts and progressive historians ever since have been happy enough to take these men at their word. But when I look back at the preceding colonial era, I see something else: a system of husbandry that was low in productivity but diverse, well suited to the landscape, and sustainable.

Colonial New England husbandry surely had its shortcomings. There is little evidence of legume rotations, of grazing management that could maintain pasture, or of any effective means to redress the acidic state of the soil. In short, they understood manure, but the magic of clover wasn't working for these guys. But by no means was this wasteful, extensive farming that stripped the forest, exhausted the soil, and moved on. That came later. American agricultural history has always involved a complex internal tension between the agrarian traditions of caring for land and building communities, and the imperatives of market capitalism. In colonial New England, we may have one of the few instances where social and ecological restraints were sufficiently strong and market opportunities sufficiently weak to keep some kind of practical and moral lid on the most destructive aspects of the drive for wealth.

NOTES

1. The reader may find useful illustrations and tables on-line at http://people.brandeis.edu/~bdonahue/GM (accessed March 17, 2008).
2. Timothy Dwight, *Travels in New England and New York* (Cambridge, Mass.: Harvard University Press, 1969), 1:76. The most likely author of *American Husbandry* was the English agricultural improver Arthur Young, who never set foot in America. See *American Husbandry*, ed. Harry J. Carman (New York: Columbia University Press, 1939).
3. Percy W. Bidwell, "The Agricultural Revolution in New England," *American Historical Review* 26 (1921): 683–702; Winifred Barr Rothenberg, *From Market-Places to a Market Economy: The Transformation of Rural Massachusetts, 1750–1850* (Chicago: University of Chicago Press, 1994).
4. William Cronon, *Changes in the Land: Indians, Colonists, and the Ecology of New England* (New York: Hill & Wang, 1983); Carolyn Merchant, *Ecological Revolutions: Nature, Gender, and Science in New England* (Chapel Hill: University of North Carolina Press, 1989).
5. Brian Donahue, "'Dammed at Both Ends and Cursed in the Middle': The 'Flowage' of the Concord River Meadows, 1798–1862," *Environmental Review* 13 (1989) 47–67; Brian Donahue, "The Forests and Fields of Concord: An Ecological History, 1750–1850," in *Concord: The Social History of a New England Town, 1750–1850*, ed. David Hackett Fischer (Waltheim, Mass.: Brandeis University, 1983); Brian Donahue, "Skinning the Land: Economic Growth and the Ecology of Farming in Nineteenth Century Massachusetts" (paper, American Social History Society, Chicago, November, 1988).

6. William Jones, "A Topographical Description of the Town of Concord, August 20th, 1792," Collections of the Massachusetts Historical Society, 1792, 1:237, Boston.

7. Middlesex Registry of Deeds [MRD], 1672, 4:409; MRD, 1774, 79–509.

8. MRD, Nathan Brooks Family Papers, box 14a, folder 3, 33–129, Concord Free Public Library.

9. Jared Eliot, *Essays upon Field Husbandry in New England, and Other Papers, 1748–1762*, ed. Harry J. Carman and Rexford G. Tugwell (New York: Columbia University Press, 1934), 27.

The Colonial Colleges

Forging an American Political Culture

J. David Hoeveler

Nine colleges existed in the British colonies of North America when the thirteen declared their independence from Great Britain in 1776. In New England, Puritans established Harvard in 1636 and Yale in 1701. The two others from that region, Rhode Island College (Brown) and Dartmouth College, sprang from the Great Awakening in 1765 and 1769, respectively. In the Middle Atlantic colonies, Presbyterians founded the College of New Jersey (Princeton) in 1746, and Anglicans established King's College (later Columbia) in 1754. Of the nine, only the College of Philadelphia (University of Pennsylvania), 1755, had nonsectarian origins. A group from the Dutch Reformed Church started Queen's College (Rutgers) in 1766. Anglican William and Mary, founded in 1693, alone represented the southern colonies.

All were established by Christians with religious intentions (the exception, Philadelphia, came quickly under Anglican and Presbyterian domination), and all were Protestant. All led their students though a curriculum heavily concentrated in the ancient languages and history, with philosophy, science, and rhetoric also prominent. Closer inspection, however, finds that the colleges reflected the diversity within American colonial religion and the factional politics it produced. The colleges were born "political," and their early intellectual histories both reflected and reinforced the religious politics of colonial America.

Six of these institutions had Calvinist beginnings. Harvard was the school of the Massachusetts Bay Puritans, operating within a decade of their arrival to New England in 1630. But by the end of the century, Harvard had come under liberal religious influence, much of it Anglican, and to the great disaffection of the orthodox Mathers and others had selected John Leverett as president in 1707. By that time, in Connecticut, a party from the orthodox group had established Yale, located first in Saybrook, in 1701. It did so with Increase Mather's blessing. But little was certain in the early collegiate history of this country. In 1722 a shocked New England learned that a group of Yale people, led by Samuel Johnson, had announced its intention to seek ordination in the hated Church of England. Johnson's education in Anglicanism had proceeded from his reading of books—English religious writings, science, and literature—that had arrived at Yale in 1714.

Establishing Princeton was the achievement of Calvinist Presbyterians. The College of New Jersey was the first to come from the religious movement known as the Great Awakening. That movement, in fact, served as a kind of political fault line for all the colonial colleges. Harvard and Yale had both given the awakeners a rude reception, so now they sought a college of their own. Factionalism in the Dutch Reformed Church during the Great Awakening also led to the founding of Queen's College in New Brunswick, New Jersey.

Earlier, news of the new Presbyterian school at Princeton had spurred the New York legislature, with New York City and powerful Anglicans in the lead, to look for a college establishment of their own. King's College resulted but only after a war of words between Anglicans and their rivals in the city. The legislation that established King's did not make it an Anglican college, so partisans had to work quickly to give it that identity. They did so when the socially influential Trinity Church bequeathed land to the new school. The trustees then named Samuel Johnson, by now colonial Anglicanism's foremost apologist, as its first president.

The Awakening would eventually yield four colonial colleges. In addition to Princeton and Queen's, Calvinists founded Rhode Island College and Dartmouth. That superficial identity, however, belies an intense and ongoing religious politics. Many of the awakeners in New England became Baptists, having concluded, as did Isaac Backus, for example, that infant baptism had no scriptural foundations. The antipaedobaptists founded new churches, all the while facing discriminatory laws in Massachusetts and Connecticut. Baptists secured their collegiate foothold with the establishment of Rhode Island College. Separatist Congregationalists, who recognized no ecclesiastical establishment and looked back to the alleged purity of the independent churches in early New England, founded Dartmouth College in Hanover, New Hampshire.

The Colonial Colleges

The early institutional histories reflect the connections between college and state. The colleges owed their legal standing to their respective colonial governments or to the British Crown, which granted them their charters. Those connections surfaced more than occasionally in the early records of these schools. Thus the Massachusetts General Court in 1699 approved a new charter with a residency law designed to remove Increase Mather from the Harvard presidency. At William and Mary, James Blair, president of that college for no less than fifty years, established a record of hardball politics in Williamsburg that led to the removal of three Virginia governors. At Princeton, Presbyterians had to use their influence against a reluctant Anglican governor to secure their charter. At Yale, President Thomas Clap, determined to resist the incursions of the Awakeners in New Haven, went to the Connecticut legislature to get a law passed against itinerant ministers; some of them had recently captured the interest of Yale students. At the College of Philadelphia, Anglican provost William Smith effected a record of political intervention and intrigue unmatched by any of his collegiate peers. He never shied from taking on the Quaker oligarchy, repeatedly allying himself with the proprietary party in the complicated mix of Pennsylvania politics. Smith paid a price for his exploits. The Quakers put him in prison! A happier political alliance prevailed in the founding of Dartmouth. That story revolved around the unlikely match between the antiestablishment leader Eleazar Wheelock and the pinnacle of the New Hampshire political dynasty, the Anglican governor John Wentworth.

The study of politics or political theory did not have a formal place in the college curriculums. Over the years, however, there developed at the colonial schools a kind of subsidiary curriculum outside the daily classroom instruction. It had three sources and immense influence. One source derived from books contributed by friends of the colleges. We see the effects most significantly at Yale, with the Jeremiah Dummer collection in 1714 and the George Berkeley donation offered in 1733. At Harvard, tutors William Brattle and William Leverett, who began teaching in 1685, brought in books from England. These collections had a liberalizing effect. The English works challenged Puritan Calvinism, they brought students up to date in modern science, and they likely exposed them to the English Whig political thinkers.

Politics also figured heavily in another part of the "extracurriculum": the student theses. The reading of theses by students at annual commencement exercises dates far back in Harvard's history. By the middle of the eighteenth century, this practice had assumed a marked political content. The theses asked and answered such questions as, "Is unlimited obedience to rulers taught by Christ and His Apostles?" (1729), "Is the Voice of the People the Voice of God?" (1733), "Is it Lawful to resist the Supreme Magistrate, if the Commonwealth cannot otherwise be preserved?" (1743), and, a popular topic that reflects Hobbesian and certainly Lockean influence, "Does Civil Government Originate from Compact?" (1743, 1747, 1751, 1761, 1762).

Third, at mid-century we find another interesting departure. Colonial students began to form their own societies, apparently seeking, in some cases, to take up current subjects outside their formal assignments. The Flat Hat Club appeared at William and Mary in 1750 and the Critonian and Linonian at Yale the same decade. Most famous were the two at Princeton: the American Whig and the Cliosophic, both established in 1765. These two organizations established an intense rivalry with satire and ad hominem aspersions abounding. James Madison at Princeton, a member and possibly a founder of the Whigs, at first pursued his love of literature and writing through his membership, but along the way a greater interest in politics emerged, and after Princeton it became his consuming focus.

These clubs were still forming on the eve of the American Revolution. And in fact, the colonial college—all of them—became heavily caught up in that great event. What stands out thematically in this history is the appearance of nine patriotic schools, including even the two Anglican ones. Some fell easily into the American cause, others with some tension and difficulty. We note, however, that in 1760, on the news of King George II's death, the six colleges then in existence all memorialized the departed monarch. Thirteen years later, American collegians wore homespun to signal their support of the American boycotts of British goods. At some schools, students formed their own militias, drilling on the college premises. And the war came to the colleges. Seven of the nine would have to suspend instruction as British or American troops took over their buildings.

The contribution of the colleges to an emerging political culture in America, though, had already begun. The revolutionary years would continue it. Reference here is made to the political leaders that these schools produced. For them, the collegiate experience laid foundations that expanded into patriot ideology and public service. A few examples suggest how this was so.

Samuel Adams came from a prosperous Boston family. He took his entrance examination at Harvard, from which he graduated in 1740, by reading passages from Tully and Virgil. For his M.A., he read John Locke, Samuel von Pufendorf, and James Harrington. This training does not suggest the fiery populist leader that Adams became for the Sons of Liberty, the simple republican known to history. But at Harvard, Adams witnessed and came to admire the religious Awakening. He praised its participants for their rejection of finery and their donning of the "somber dress" of the old Puritans. When Adams took up political journalism after his graduation, his earnest writing expressed his fears of material corruption in Britain and America, citing the historical example of Rome and its trajectory from moral republic to decadent empire. Adams, a familiar face in the Boston taverns, came to respect the common people and their common ways; he became known for his "genteel poverty." Adams's religious Puritanism and his classical education together forged the model of a "Christian Sparta" that he held up for his fellow colonialists. Many described Adams as the Cato of the American Revolution.

Younger cousin John Adams entered Harvard with no intellectual interests at all. College changed him profoundly. He would cite as a special influence his studies with Harvard scientist John Winthrop IV, which led Adams in the direction of liberal Christianity. He may have rejected the Calvinism of some clergy he knew, but he came to appreciate the Puritans and their earlier struggles against the tyranny of monarchy and church in the Stuart era. Shifting from a possible career in the pulpit to one in law, Adams, with some Boston colleagues, formed the Sodalitas Club. Its members proposed to study law and oratory and met Thursday evenings to discuss a selected legal text from a list of classic works. Adams's political ideas crystallized when the group examined feudal law. He presented his ideas to the club and then offered them to the world in his noted publication, his *Dissertation on the Canon and Feudal Law,* one of the major documents in the literature of the American Revolution. Harvard's rational Christianity shone through in Adams's harsh judgments of the "superstitions" that were the props of kingship and ecclesiastical oppression. Adams described the Protestant Reformation as an intellectual advance, to which his ancestral Puritans contributed. He also celebrated the Puritans for their fight against English tyranny. Adams also found instruction in ancient history, as his subsequent writings reveal. History, for him, was always a lesson book, informed by his classical education at Harvard. For every contemporary situation, it seemed, Adams could find an instructive analogy in ancient Greece and Rome.

Yale College made its connections to the Revolution through a different route. The neo-Calvinist movement known as the "New Divinity" was based in rural Connecticut, and its major advocates were Yale graduates. Samuel Hopkins, later a prominent clergyman in Newport, Rhode Island, and Joseph Bellamy, of Bethel, Connecticut, linked religion and politics in their preaching and writing. They shared with other Protestant leaders in America a conviction that not England alone but the colonies, too, had lapsed into the material comforts of empire (Hopkins strongly attacked the slave trade and the Americans' connection to it) and stood sorely in need of a moral and spiritual recovery. Hopkins hoped that the Revolution would supply that need. Bellamy, in turn, associated liberal religion (Arminianism had always been a theological heresy at orthodox Yale) with high, fashionable living. By the middle of the 1770s, Bellamy and others in the New Divinity party were urging Americans to swear off all British imports, the luxury and finery of a bloated empire, one that Bellamy judged "ripe for destruction."

Harvard's and Yale's Puritan roots explain much about their opposition to England in the Revolutionary era. Princeton College drew also on New England and Scotch-Irish foundations, and even before the arrival of John Witherspoon from Scotland in 1768, it had evidenced nationalist sentiments. Princeton outpaced all the colonial colleges in supplying leaders for the new nation, with James Madison being the most noteworthy. He reflects, through his education under Witherspoon, an evident connection to the Scottish Enlightenment. Witherspoon had brought with him to the College of New Jersey his own collection of Scottish works, including those of David Hume, Adam Ferguson, John Millar, and Adam Smith. They directly influenced Madison's part in reconstructing American political thought, contributing new ideas about republicanism in the large-state setting and the role of factions in that arena. Those ideas, of course, had their most succinct expression in Madison's famous tenth *Federalist* essay.

In the making of patriot colleges, the two Anglican schools supply the most surprising twists. One would expect the College of William and Mary and King's College to embody loyalist attachments to the British Crown. And indeed such feelings flourished among many at these institutions. At Williamsburg, however, a young Thomas Jefferson graduated and reinforced his college studies with lawyer George Wythe, reading Francis Hutcheson, Lord Kames, John Locke, Algernon Sidney, and Sir Edward Coke and deriving much of the intellectual ammunition for his revolutionary politics. James Madison [later Bishop Madison and no relation to the above] supplies another striking example. At William and Mary in 1773, the young Anglican had become professor of science immediately upon his graduation from the college. Madison's speeches, beginning in his undergraduate years, reverberated with Whig notions, especially Locke's. The William and Mary curriculum had created its own subversions of its loyalist identity.

And King's College, which had in President Myles Cooper an unabashed Loyalist, also contributed to the patriotic cause. Three King's collegians—John Jay, Gouverneur Morris, and Alexander Hamilton—represented a group labeled the "Conservative Whigs" in New York politics. Hamilton had electrified New York City audiences with his powerful attacks on the British and in 1774 and 1775, barely more than twenty years old, he engaged the Loyalist Samuel Seabury in a remarkable pamphlet exchange that furnished some of the most interesting political literature of the day. Hamilton drew on the compact theory of government and insisted that oppressive British action had dissolved the American connection. He also drew on William Blackstone to advance a theory of natural law.

College presidents by no means shunned the political arena, and often they charged into it with all their polemical weapons at hand. John Witherspoon at Princeton furnishes the fullest portrait of the activist president. In Princeton, he entertained travelers, such as John Adams and Richard Henry Lee, who were on their way to the Continental Congress in Philadelphia. Ultimately he could not deny himself the opportunity to go there himself. Witherspoon became the only clergyman to sign the Declaration of Independence. After some hesitation, he brought revolutionary politics to the college campus. His pronunciation in "The Dominion of Providence over the Passions of Men" stands as a major piece in the sermon literature of the American Revolution. Witherspoon, though, went even further. When New Jersey insurgents moved against Loyalist governor William Franklin, they hauled him before the New Jersey Provincial Council. Witherspoon served as grand inquisitor for the proceedings.

Harvard and Yale also provided revolutionary presidents. Samuel Langdon had arrived from his pulpit in Portsmouth, New Hampshire, to his new office at Harvard in 1774. Just six weeks after the fighting at Lexington and Concord the next year, he gave a sermon at Harvard, one thematically rich in its references to ancient Israel, the decay of the British Constitution, the oppression of the current regime in England, and, yes, America's own sin. Langdon urged the need to recover a more strictly biblical Christianity. At Yale, graduate Ezra Stiles had moved over to a ministry in Newport, then to Portsmouth, and back to Yale as its president in 1778. He had already become the leader among other American ministers—Congregationalists and Presbyterians mostly—in their organizing efforts against appointment of an Anglican bishop to the colonies. Indeed, the first two meetings of this Plan of Union, in 1767 and 1768, took place on the Yale campus. There, in the late 1770s, Stiles cheered the American cause at every turn and detailed in his diary the dramatic events of the British advance onto New Haven in the summer of 1779.

In the overall pattern, the older Puritan schools—Harvard and Yale—thus became readily patriotic. So, too, did the two New Jersey schools born of the religious Awakening—Princeton and Queen's. The Baptist leaders at

Rhode Island College, however, had mixed feelings. They saw only hypocrisy in the libertarian rhetoric of New Englanders who defended their rights against British tyranny all the while denying full equality to the Baptists in their midst. Rhode Island College president James Manning went to the second convention meeting in Philadelphia to win a resolution supporting the Baptists against New England's Standing Order. He had no success. At Dartmouth, in turn, President Wheelock's patriotic feelings confronted the political realities of his alliance with Governor Wentworth, an Anglican. He tried in vain to forge a reconciliation between patriots and English. His compromising efforts only aroused his critics, and he left office a heartsick man.

Finally, at the College of Philadelphia, Provost William Smith, an Anglican, promised loyalty to the American cause but convinced few. Vice-Provost Francis Alison, Presbyterian, led the American cause, the coleader, with Stiles, in the anti-Anglican Plan of Union. This college ultimately furnished the fullest case of state intervention in the revolutionary years. The Supreme Executive Council, created by the new Pennsylvania constitution, turned on the college trustees, citing their expressions of British loyalty, and it named Smith specifically as one of forty-one offenders. In 1779 the radical party in the state, dominated by Presbyterians, reconfigured the college. Benjamin Franklin, whom Smith had earlier driven from the trustees, now returned and resumed his position at the college, renamed by the state legislature the University of Pennsylvania.

The literature of the American Revolution, in the colleges and outside them, drew from many sources—Calvinism, the ancient classics, Whig ideology, the Scottish Enlightenment. But in its many expressions, that literature unfolded within the precise contexts of nine institutional histories. Therefore, no simple pattern prevailed. As with the thirteen colonies themselves, the colonial colleges forged an ostensible unity and shaped an American political culture. It was never an ideology and not a hegemony. Each college made its individual contribution to the pluralist American Mind.

Groping for National Identity by Forging a National Cuisine

James E. McWilliams

The first generation of white Americans to come of age after the American Revolution had to perform a cultural balancing act. On the one hand, it had to forge a unique identity, one that disassociated the new republic from timeworn habits. The process of establishing a national persona was multifaceted and not easily summarized, but in general it required Americans to embrace the most conspicuous difference between their nascent society and the established customs of the motherland: the comparative "wildness" of the American environment. Charles Woodmason, an itinerant minister working in the 1750s, did more than echo empty rhetoric when he described himself as negotiating "the Wild Woods of America." For better or worse, he highlighted early America's roughhewn environment as its most telling point of distinction from Great Britain, which had effectively served as a prevailing role model.

On the other hand, though, while young Americans eagerly sought to highlight the wooly virtues of their mythical frontier, they had to do so without tipping their praise too far in the "culture of wilderness" direction. An overzealous advocacy of the "Wild Woods," after all, would have risked endorsing the world view of the "savages"—the indigenous population that Anglo-Americans worked so diligently to dispossess and banish. To be sure, urgent political and diplomatic matters animated public life in the early republic—writing a constitution, staying out of war, fighting a war, avoiding secession, to name a few examples—and they all contributed to the process of national-identity construction. But the pervasive challenge of juggling European refinement and Native American primitiveness persisted as an ongoing if subtle cultural concern that, in one way or another, touched the lives of every white American. The threat of going native, balanced against the threat of falling into overcivilized luxury, consistently tempered early Americans' efforts to conceptualize their national character.

While scholarly approaches to understanding this dilemma are potentially endless, American culinary habits provide an especially clear lens through which to capture early Americans struggling with this important cultural negotiation. By the time of the American Revolution, America's diverse culinary landscape had coalesced into a rough but vaguely definable "American" mode of eating. Intensely regional cuisines, whose differences were further intensified by racial and ethnic contributions—not to mention radically different environmental conditions—had gently converged by the early nineteenth century. They did so under the influence of increasing coastal trade and a homogenizing consumer revolution that started to standardize material life, especially in the kitchen. These factors eventually helped early Americans pioneer a diet based on what they saw as the frontier virtues of simplicity, self-sufficiency, pragmatism, and a measured lack of pretension. By the early nineteenth century, American cookbooks, while not necessarily pouring off the presses, were nonetheless becoming useful items in American kitchens and, more importantly, offering middle-class women accessible recipes written, as a popular example put it, "in the American mode."

One can, in short, identify at least a vague emergence of something that historians are only beginning to explore in real depth: American food. And it turns out that cooking and eating, perhaps more than other cultural endeavors, provided early Americans with an accessible means to define and perpetuate their new, if amorphous, national identity. Food, in short, provided Americans a venue to figure out who they were.

Understanding the power of food as a cultural arbiter in the new republic requires insight into its colonial history. In the light of the larger culinary trends that developed in British America, the post-Revolutionary unifying influence of food comes as something of a surprise. A survey of the diverse diets that evolved throughout the eighteenth century, after all, reveals regional habits deeply embroidered into extremely different environmental, cultural, and agricultural backgrounds. These backgrounds, by virtue of their diversity, seemed to have little chance of finding common ground.

On one end of the North American spectrum, New England strove to replicate the culinary habits of idealized English traditions. The region's adaptation of mixed agriculture, the presence of geographical conditions that impeded the production of staple crops, and a population comprising prosperous middle-class settlers all enhanced the widespread effort to embrace inherited customs and eat like proper English families. Typical households settled on modestly sized plantations, grew vegetable gardens and orchards, kept livestock for beef and dairy, seeded their fields with English clover grass, and cultivated as much English wheat, rye, and oats as precious labor and ample land would allow. Mixed farming demanded little foreign labor—certainly few slaves—and required minimal interaction with indigenous peoples. With their comparatively open access to the metropolis and relatively high literacy rates, New Englanders were also more likely than other colonists to import and rely on directives found in English cookbooks and farming manuals. Their successful approximation of English ways—in matters culinary as well as others—stands as one the region's greatest accomplishments. It's an accomplishment, moreover, that made their diet as familiar as it could have been in a strange new world.

On the other end of the culinary spectrum, the Lower South pioneered habits that reflected a nearly complete abandonment of traditional English eating customs. An overwhelming emphasis on extensive rice cultivation, a white population with little interest in replicating English habits, a heavy reliance on slave labor, and routine interaction with Native American cultures led to a way of eating that many Europeans characterized as something just shy of barbaric. But not so the Carolinians. It was in the Deep South, for example, where colonists were more likely to tolerate and even embrace meals deriving from the indigenous population with whom southerners routinely dealt. "We were entertained," John Lawson, the English surveyor of Carolina, wrote, "with a fat boiled goose, venison, raccoon, and ground nuts." On another occasion, Lawson consumed a stew made by "Congree Indians" that consisted of "3 teal and a possum," politely pronouncing the dish "a curious ragoo." Despite the "curious" nature of the local cuisine, however, Lawson and other plantation-owning Carolinians willingly adopted many of its "wild" characteristics, noting that settlers were "never wanting of a good appetite" so long as they relied on "the adjacent woods" and rivers "well-stored with fish." It's hard to imagine a proper New Englander entertaining these victuals with such flexible open-mindedness.

The region's strong adherence to slavery further distinguished southern eating habits from those of the motherland and New England. With African Americans constituting a majority of the population (in some places reaching 90 percent), and with masters granting slaves land to grow their own crops (it was cheaper than importing food), African-based culinary traditions inevitably rose from the bottom up. Writing about "Guinea Corn," for example, the naturalist Mark Catesby noted how it was "propagated, and that chiefly by the negroes, who make a bread of it, and boil it in the manner of firmity." Once again, in terms of food, Carolina could not have been more different from New England.

Other regions of British America fell between these extremes. They did so, however, while developing their own distinguishing features. The Middle Colonies—Pennsylvania, in particular—leaned in the New England direction. It developed a cuisine commensurate with an economy based on extensive wheat and dairy farming, an ethnically diverse population, a multifaceted labor force that included slaves and servants, and an intricately connected urban-rural network of exchange. These factors combined with the region's Quaker-inspired foundation to support a mode of eating that stressed frugality and flexibility, inspiring a diet that was measured but diverse, reliant on beef, cheese, and bread but readily open to pork, scrapple, or corn mush. The Chesapeake Bay region—Virginia especially—hewed closer to the Carolina model. Settlers there fashioned a cuisine that reflected the region's overwhelming emphasis on tobacco, servants, and slaves. Extensive quantities of salted pork, corn meal, wild game, and occasional supplies of vegetables and fruit allowed English colonists to approximate some aspects of traditional English cuisine while remaining comparatively dependent on the "wild woods" for food, thus reflecting the habits of their cohorts down south.

A distinct medley of cuisines and one that's still recognizable to this day thus made up the foodways of British America. While these original modes of diet persisted, however, a more cohesive American way of eating emerged in the years just preceding the American Revolution. The reason for this convergence centered on two main factors: the rise in intercoastal trade and the increasing availability of British goods. Intercoastal commercial activity developed in large part on the back of the rum and molasses trade that burgeoned between the mainland and Barbados after 1720. As merchants ferried these highly demanded goods up and down the East Coast, they began to trade foodstuffs as well. By the 1750s it was more possible than it had ever been for British Americans to enjoy food from other regions. Okra, for example, made its way to Rhode Island. Virginia ham found a market in South Carolina. New England cod went to the Middle Colonies. Pennsylvania sent pork and butter throughout the colonies. These few examples only scratch the surface of an expanding commercial trend. By the 1770s, as the Revolution approached, regional ingredients had become, as a result of the increasingly systematic nature of intercolonial trade, much less limited to their respective regions. An intercolonial food exchange, in short, was underway.

Complementing this rising availability of what had once been strictly local ingredients was the growing uniformity of the colonial cooking experience.

Utensils, recipes, and kitchen space throughout British America began to look increasingly alike. The reasons had to do with supply, demand, and cultural imperatives. "It is really possible," wrote a German visitor to the colonies in the 1750s, "to obtain all the things one can get in Europe in Pennsylvania." This observer was speaking in reference to a commercial trend that historians have gone so far as to call a consumer revolution, and, although he was speaking of Philadelphia, he could just as easily been referring to New York, Charleston, Boston, Newport, or Baltimore. With rising colonial incomes and declining prices of English durable goods, Americans after 1730 radically improved their standard of living to include, among other luxuries, expanded kitchens stocked with new stoves and English cooking tools, tables, chairs, and cookbooks. This material transformation allowed English colonists to act upon a cultural influence that had nagged them throughout the colonial era. They could, that is, finally approximate metropolitan life with some accuracy—something they had always wanted to do. As Benjamin Franklin put it in the late 1760s, colonists "had not only a respect, but an affection, for Great Britain, for its laws, its customs, and manners." He could also have accurately added "its food." Ironically, as the eve of the American Revolution approached, colonists were actively enjoying access to more ingredients as well as the English accoutrements that enabled them to Anglicize and refine—however modestly—the relatively rugged cuisine of which they were often ashamed.

But the American Revolution posed an unexpected problem. For all the colonists' success in replicating English eating habits during the consumer revolution, the Revolution ended the transition from provincial backwardness to metropolitan sophistication. Just when British America was beginning to feel integrated into the cultural patterns of the empire, politics intervened, and the empire imposed infringements that turned Americans into reluctant but committed revolutionaries. The victorious outcome of the American Revolution inspired political changes that rapidly redefined America—despite its 750,000 slaves—as the pinnacle of liberty. We have studied this transition thoroughly. Lost in our heavy emphasis on political transformation, however, is a profound cultural problem that had tremendous implications for the young American identity. The United States had a general idea what its new political system would look like. It had no idea, however, what its new cultural values would be. In suggestive ways, colonists turned to food to seek answers.

Americans used food to strike the balance between refinement and ruggedness. Promoting his play *The Father,* William Dunlap advertised the production as "a frugal plain repast" in contrast to the "high seasoned food" dished out by European dramatists. This description was more than an empty advertising slogan. Indeed, in America, thoughts about proper food clearly came to stress frugality, roughness, flexibility, and a radical openness to experimentation. American food, like the American people, was mythologized to be pragmatic, self-sufficient, adaptable, and without artifice. Whether any of this was actually the case is beside the point. But the fact that Americans began consciously to promote their food as a contrast to the excessive refinement of European cuisine highlights a critical aspect of national-identity formation. Whereas many colonists, especially those in the northern colonies, had spent much of the colonial era trying to downplay British America's rugged (and thus provincial) character, early Americans now began to embrace it, although in a much more controlled fashion than they once had. Few white Americans (including southerners) were willing to champion the extreme culinary examples provided by the rural south. Nevertheless, the fact remained that early Americans, consciously or not, promoted a mode of eating that owed a lot to the tolerance and flexibility enabling southerners to accept Native American and African influences on their diet and, in turn, transform English-inherited practices into American culinary creations. At the same time, they eschewed the refinement that New Englanders had long sought without (again, the goal was to strike a balance) fully rejecting it.

Instances of early Americans achieving this balance appeared in unlikely places and at unlikely times. Yet they occurred frequently enough to form a pattern. Patrick Henry, the great Revolutionary agitator, condemned Thomas Jefferson's predilection for fine French food, warning him never to "abjure his native victuals." Years later, in 1840, William Henry Harrison slandered his presidential opponent, Martin Van Buren, by informing the electorate that Van Buren had an affinity not for simple American food but rather for soup *a la reine* and pate de fois gras. European visitors to the early republic remarked repeatedly on the dining habits and attitudes of young Americans in ways that suggested the Americans' proud adherence to a pragmatic mode of eating. The Duke of Liancourt wrote with astonishment about how easily Americans accepted Indian corn into their diet. It was, he explained, "the national crop . . . eaten three times a day." In rural areas, he went on, "fresh meat could not regularly be got, except in the shape of poultry or game; but the hog cost nothing to keep, and very little to kill and preserve. Thus the ordinary American was brought up on salt pork and Indian corn, or rye." Thomas Ashe in his *Travels in America in 1806* observed that Americans had no problem with salted meat, telling how one timber worker he met opined, "Your fresh meat, that's too fancy." Even Charles Dickens, on a trip to the

United States in the 1830s, commented on America's culinary pragmatism, writing about how he consumed a fine spread of "tea, coffee, bread, butter, salmon, shad, liver, steak, potatoes, pickles, ham, chops, black-puddings, and sausages" but that "dinner was breakfast again without the tea and coffee; and supper and breakfast were identical."

These examples, with their deeply suggestive culinary opinions, show Americans walking a fine line between European refinement and provincial ruggedness and, in essence, defining their broader culture. Without consciously doing so, Americans were drawing on two deeply ingrained elements of their diverse culinary heritage to forge a national identity that served them well as they moved west, confronted new "wild" territories, and worked to "subdue the wilderness." The ruggedness of the colonial frontier, a characteristic of North America that British Americans once associated with the indigenous population, became an aspect that early Americans could now, with the British model dissipating, embrace with measured enthusiasm. Likewise, the refinement of the idealized English (and European) diet was now a quality that young Americans could overtly condemn (rather than, as they once had, praise) without completely dismissing its welcome trappings. Through the virtues that American food embraced—frugality, simplicity, pragmatism, unpretentiousness—the United States could grow into a sophisticated nation while avoiding the enervating habit of complacency into which the British had fallen. It could announce, as Thomas Jefferson did, "how unripe we yet are," all the while knowing that ripeness, like an overly refined cuisine, was something to avoid. Most important, they could strike this balance by growing, cooking, and eating food.

PART 3

Revolution and the Early Republic

Local Authority and the Origins of the U.S. Constitution

Gordon S. Wood

In 1989, at the two hundredth anniversary of the founding of the U.S. Congress, I gave a lecture at the Library of Congress on the origins of the Congress. During the question period, a woman very angrily asked, "Why don't you historians of the founders give proper credit to the Iroquois in the creation of the Constitution?" I had never heard of this Iroquois contribution. I should have, I suppose, because I later discovered that during the previous year, in October 1988, the House of Representatives and the Senate had passed resolutions thanking the Iroquois for their contribution to the framing of the United States Constitution. Laura Nader was this woman's name. She's the sister of Ralph Nader and a professor of anthropology at the University of California, Berkeley. She was so angry she wrote a letter to the James Billington, Librarian of Congress, enclosing an article by another anthropologist, and suggested that Billington send this to Wood and educate him in the origins of the Constitution. So Billington sent it on to me.

This is how the anthropological argument roughly goes. Benjamin Franklin was at the Albany Congress in 1754 and, diplomat that he was, congratulated the Iroquois on their ability to bring five tribes together to form the Confederacy of the Iroquois Nation. Then three decades later at the Constitutional Convention in 1787, Franklin presumably passed this idea of confederation on to his fellow delegates at Philadelphia, and in this manner the Iroquois influenced the creation of the Constitution.

This essay is adapted from a plenary address Professor Wood gave April 13, 2007, in Williamsburg, Virginia, at "Expanding Horizons: Individuals and Their Encounters with the New," the annual conference of the National Council for History Education. The essay appeared in *Historically Speaking* 8 (July/August 2007).

This curious notion of causality doesn't quite work. The Iroquois and the other Indians certainly contributed a great deal to early American culture. But ideas about federalism and the dividing and parceling out of political power were not among their contributions. The framers in 1787 did not have to borrow such ideas from the Iroquois. The English colonists had their own long tradition of dividing up and parceling out power from the bottom up; the framers knew all by themselves how to draw up confederated governments. The origins of American federalism and American localism went back at least to the early seventeenth-century English settlements in Virginia and New England.

The migrants who settled Jamestown and the Chesapeake and later New England came already primed with a long English heritage of local autonomy. As the populations in both the Chesapeake area and in New England quickly dispersed, this acute English sense of local authority was reinforced and intensified. No one had quite expected such rapid dispersion. The Virginia Company, for example, hoped to set up boroughs in the Chesapeake and, indeed, created four towns on paper—Jamestown, Charles City, Henrico, and Kiccowtan. The settlers' desire to grow tobacco, a very soil-exhausting crop, undid the plan of having boroughs with burgesses as citizens. Although only one of the four towns, Jamestown, actually arose, the colony's legislature was initially called the House of Burgesses, and the name stuck.

Instead of congregating in towns, the settlers dispersed and created private plantations throughout the Chesapeake area. By 1622 the spread of the population was such that not all of the judicial cases could be brought to Jamestown. And so the magistrates, that is, the members of the governor's council, went on circuit to hear judicial cases. By 1632 the authorities created five monthly courts, each headed by one of the magistrates. By 1634 the scattering of settlements had become so great in the Chesapeake area that some sort of local organization became necessary, and the colony was divided into eight counties, in imitation of England's county structure, each with its own court.

Within less than a generation of settlement, these county courts became not only the basic unit of local government in Virginia but also the source of representation in the central government, with each county sending two burgesses to the central government. Although the parish originally had been the organization for local government, the county soon supplanted it and became the sole authority relating to the central authority in Jamestown. The county courts became powerful, self-perpetuating bodies that combined within themselves various civil, criminal, ecclesiastical, admiralty, and administrative jurisdictions that in England were exercised by different institutions. They assumed the power to deal with orphans, probate wills, collect taxes, regulate morals, supervise the militia, maintain prices, relieve the poor, issue land titles, license taverns, control the parish vestries—in fact, the men sitting on the vestries tended to be the same men sitting on the county court—and to enact bylaws for their counties.

The same dispersion of people and localization of authority took place in New England. Within three months of landing in 1630, the Puritans had created seven towns surrounding Boston. These New England towns became the sole unit of local government. Like the Chesapeake county courts, the town united within itself a host of powers that had been widely shared by different local institutions in England. The parish, the borough, the village, the manor court, the county—all were collapsed into the New England town.

In England the Crown was considered to be the source of all local authority. But during the first generation of settlement in the New World, the English Crown for all intents and purposes simply did not exist. This meant that the local units of government in both the Chesapeake and New England attained extraordinary degrees of autonomy and power without being beholden to the Crown at all. Indeed, so strong and autonomous did the local authorities become that even the central governments in each of the early colonies in the Chesapeake and New England had difficulty dealing with them.

It soon became evident that these central authorities not only often existed at the behest or the sufferance of the local units but also were sometimes the creatures of the local units. The colony of Connecticut, for example, was created in 1639 when three independent towns—Hartford, Windsor, and Wethersfield—came together and agreed in a written Fundamental Orders to form a superintending central government (which is why Connecticut today puts "the constitution state" on its auto registration plates). These Connecticut colonists had a clear sense that they were creating a central government from the bottom up. A similar development took place in New Haven in 1643, when a half-dozen towns joined together to form a separate colony. In the 1660s these towns revolted and joined Connecticut. All this reinforced the view that authority was created by the pooling together of local power from below.

Some towns in New England sometimes belonged to no colony at all. Springfield, for example, existed independently for a decade or so until 1649, when it was finally incorporated into the colony of Massachusetts Bay. Although ostensibly a colony, seventeenth-century Rhode Island was in reality four more or less independent towns: Providence, founded by Roger Williams; Portsmouth, founded by Anne Hutchinson, in flight from the Puritans in Boston; Newport, founded by William Coddington; and Warwick, or Shawomut as it was called then, founded by a real radical, Samuel Gorton, who was as cantankerous a character as you'll ever find in American history. Williams was constantly trying to bring these cranky Puritans together, but they were at each other's throats through the whole period. Williams finally got a patent from the Puritan Parliament in 1644 and unified the towns temporarily in 1647, but that central authority remained very weak. The towns couldn't agree where the colony's government should meet, so they rotated from one town to another. In the 1650s the confederation of towns, such as it was, fell apart. Rhode Island now had two general assemblies, two sets of officials. In the end the colony was rescued by a man named John Clarke, who, unlike Roger Williams, is virtually unknown today. Although he was a Puritan, Clarke nonetheless succeeded in securing a royal charter from Charles II's government in London in 1663, three years after the ousting of the Puritans and the restoration of the Stuarts. To this day no one knows quite how he did it, but he saved the colony of Rhode Island. Yet despite the royal charter, near town anarchy continued to exist throughout the seventeenth century. The towns disregarded many laws—from collecting taxes to recording land titles—and scarcely existed as a united colony.

This intense localization of authority that took place both in New England and the Chesapeake was not matched by any corresponding clarification of the relationship between the central governments and the local governments, whether towns or counties. Plymouth Colony is a good example. It was founded in 1620 by Pilgrims who had a patent from the Virginia Company. But they landed in Cape Cod and then Plymouth, outside of the Virginia Company's claim. They realized that immediately, which is why the Pilgrims drew up the Mayflower Compact, granting them some legal authority to govern themselves. In 1621 they got a new patent from the New England Council, which soon went out of business and was superseded by the Massachusetts Bay charter of 1629. So the Pilgrims found themselves in Plymouth with no legal authority whatsoever except from a patent from a company that no longer existed. William Bradford, the great diarist—he wrote a wonderful history of Plymouth Colony that everyone should read—controlled the patent, such as it was, and ruled rather autocratically. But there were protests from the towns, which by 1640 numbered ten. As the towns scattered westward, the central authority's control over them was steadily weakened. By the 1680s the towns were in open revolt, refusing to pay taxes

Local Authority and the Origins of the Constitution

to the central government in Plymouth. When Massachusetts Bay acquired a new royal charter in 1691, it inevitably swallowed up the disintegrating Plymouth Colony.

Given this experience of creating government from the bottom up, it was natural for the colonies of New England—Massachusetts Bay, Plymouth, New Haven, and Connecticut—to come together in 1643 to form the New England Confederation (Rhode Island was too insignificant or objectionable to be included). Since this was more than a century before the Albany Conference, these New Englanders created their confederation without the help of the Iroquois. They designed their confederation to protect themselves from the Indians and from the Dutch and the French who were on their flanks. Since Massachusetts Bay tried to dominate the other colonies, the confederation was short-lived. But the idea of pooling authority from the bottom up —creating confederations—was very much a part of the early American experience.

Even the legislatures of the separate colonies were in a sense the products of the bringing together of local authorities. Both the counties in the Chesapeake and the towns in New England demanded voices in the central governments, which, at the outset, were simply the governors and their councils, usually a dozen men or so. Of course, the governors and their councils had a need to reach out to the local units, and these mutual interests of the central and local authorities led to the creation of legislatures—composed in the case of Virginia of two burgesses from each county and in the case of the New England colonies, two deputies from each town.

In those colonies where strong central and local forces pulled in opposite directions, the legislatures split apart and created bicameral assemblies. This didn't happen in Connecticut or Plymouth because the central governments in those colonies were too weak. But the central government in Massachusetts Bay was especially strong, and it resisted the centrifugal pull of the town authorities. In 1644 a series of disputes between the magistrates and the town deputies came to a head over a case involving Goody Sherman's sow. Up to then the magistrates, standing for the central authority, and the deputies, representing local interests, had met together as the General Court. In this case the court voted seventeen to fifteen in favor of Sherman, with two magistrates and fifteen deputies for Sherman and seven magistrates and eight deputies for her opponent, a merchant named Robert Keayne. The magistrates protested, contending that a majority of magistrates should have a negative over all decisions. The magistrates eventually won, and the General Court was divided into two houses, with the magistrates in one and the deputies in the other.

Virginia had a similar struggle in the 1660s that also led to a two-house legislature. Although in the eighteenth century this bicameralism was often considered to be an imitation of the English Parliament, with its House of Commons and its House of Lords, its seventeenth-century origins lay in these struggles between local and central authorities.

Yet even as eighteenth-century Americans began regarding their governments as miniature copies of the English Parliament, they continued to think of their legislative representatives in seventeenth-century terms, as in effect ambassadors from their local districts. Not only did the counties and towns often bind their agents with instructions, they sometimes refused to pay taxes if their representatives weren't present at the time the taxes were voted.

This was what the Americans came to call "actual representation," which by the eighteenth century was very different from the English conception of representation. Although the House of Commons had begun in the thirteenth century as a collection of delegates from particular towns and counties, by the eighteenth century it had come to be thought of as representing the whole commons of England, the entire estate of the people, not particular local units. Indeed, by the eighteenth century some local English places that continued to send representatives to Parliament had no populations had all; the town of Dunwich, for example, had long since fallen into the North Sea. During the imperial debate of the 1760s and 1770s, the English called their hodgepodge of representation "virtual representation."

Those contrasting ideas of representation were aspects of a larger difference of opinion over the nature of state power. Because Americans had tended to think of government as a pooling together of power from below, they never really developed, as the English did, a modern sense of state power. Because the state bureaucracy of the English Crown had never reached deeply into the colonial localities, state authority had generally remained for the colonists an extraneous and alien force; when it did touch them, as it did with the trade regulations, it was usually hostile and susceptible to corruption. Consequently Americans came to think of state power as something distant and dangerous.

Given this long colonial history of local autonomy, it was something of a miracle that Americans accepted such a strong and centralized national government as was created in 1787. But the modern state power embodied in the new federal government was much more potential than actual. Although Alexander Hamilton and the Federalists in the 1790s did attempt to create a modern European-style state, with a bureaucracy and a standing army, their efforts provoked a vigorous reaction that brought the United States in

1798–99 close to a civil war. The Federalists flew in the face of the local realities of American life and provoked a backlash that catapulted Thomas Jefferson into the presidency.

Because Jefferson allowed America's localist realities to express themselves, his election, as he later claimed, was as important a revolution as the Revolution of 1776. Jefferson dismantled most of the state apparatus that Hamilton had tried to build up. He eliminated all internal taxes and cut back the bureaucracy and the military forces. He, in effect, destroyed, for the first half of the nineteenth century at least, whatever chance there was for a European-style centralized state to be imposed on America.

Jefferson hated all bureaucracy and all coercive instruments of government. In fact, he sometimes gave the impression that government was only a device by which the few attempted to rob, cheat, and oppress the many. He certainly never accepted the modern idea of a state as an entity possessing a life of its own, distinct from both the rulers and the ruled. For Jefferson, there could be no power independent of the people at large. In place of a modern state apparatus, he wanted tiny ward republics that would involve the actual participation of people in their localities.

Not only did Jefferson refuse to recognize the structure and institutions of a modern state but he also scarcely accepted the basic premise of a state, that is, its presumed monopoly of legitimate control over a prescribed territory. During his first presidential administration, the United States was really just a loosely bound confederation, not all that different from the Articles of Confederation of the 1780s. Jefferson's vision of an expanding empire of liberty over a huge continent posed no problem for his relaxed idea of a national government. "Who can limit the extent to which the federative principle may operate effectively?" he asked in his second inaugural address. In fact, Jefferson always conceived of his empire of liberty as one of like principles, not like boundaries. As long as Americans believed certain things, he said, they remained Americans, regardless of the territory they happened to be in. At times he was remarkably indifferent to the possibility that a western confederacy might break away from the eastern United States. What did it matter? he asked in 1804. "Those of the western confederacy will be as much our children and descendents as those of the eastern."

It was Jefferson's contempt for the modern state, his extraordinary faith in the natural sociability of people as a substitute for the traditional adhesives of government, that made the Federalists, and especially Hamilton, dismiss him as a hopeless, pie-in-the-sky dreamer. Yet it was Jefferson's localism and his view of the minimal state that dominated American thinking through at least the first half of the nineteenth century. In fact, most Americans in that period only felt the presence of the federal government through the delivery of the mail.

Of course, all this has now changed. We've discovered that the national government created by the founders in 1787, especially the presidency, was latently very powerful. Indeed, compared to many federal governments that now exist—Canada, Australia, and Germany—the United States is one of the strongest and most centralized. But as powerful and centralized as the American federal government has become, it still operates in a culture that profoundly mistrusts distant, centralized, political power. A long tradition of local authority, deeply rooted in the earliest experiences of the American people, still affects the character of American political life. When former Speaker of the House Tip O'Neill declared that all American politics is local, everyone knew what he meant—435 representatives speaking for their local constituencies were not easily brought together. We all sense that it is the American people in their separate localities that ultimately matter and that any superior centralized authority set over them is a kind of temporary delegation from these localities. This intense sense of localism is the product of the historical experience of those original settlers that began four hundred years ago.

An Interview with John Ferling

Conducted by Joseph S. Lucas

JOSEPH S. LUCAS: During your long and productive career, you have bucked several of the trends that have defined your generation of historians. You have focused on elite leaders rather than marginalized masses. Your primary concerns are political and military history rather than social and cultural history. And you see the past not as a foreign country but as intimately connected to the present. Indeed, you argue that the past, particularly with regard to political and military leadership, holds important lessons for us today. How do you account for your iconoclastic views? And how do you see your work in relation to that of your peers and colleagues?

JOHN FERLING: Well, for many years I had a poster over my desk, and it contained a quote from Henry David Thoreau about marching to a different drummer. So maybe I am iconoclastic. But I don't think so. I think I've wound up doing what I've done out of necessity because of where I teach. It just seems the pragmatic thing to do. I don't teach at a major research university, and I don't have a research library at my disposal. So I've chosen to work with the resources available to me on a daily basis. We have things like the modern editions of the Washington papers, Franklin papers, Hamilton papers, Adams papers, and so forth. That was the direction that I went simply because the material was there and available to me. As a result, I think, most of my work has been on political and military history.

John Ferling, professor emeritus of history at the State University of West Georgia (he retired in May 2004), has written extensively on the political and military history of early America. Among his recent works are *Almost a Miracle: The American Victory in the War of Independence* (2007), *Adams vs. Jefferson: The Tumultuous Election of 1800* (2004), *A Leap in the Dark: The Struggle to Create the American Republic* (2003), and *Setting the World Ablaze: Washington, Adams, Jefferson, and the American Revolution* (2000). Joseph S. Lucas interviewed this prolific student of early American history in April of 2004. From *Historically Speaking* 6 (September/October 2004).

When I was finishing graduate school, I had a one-year appointment at a school just outside of Philadelphia in Chester County. I was very much interested in abolitionism, and there was a wonderful library of abolitionist materials in Chester County, maybe five minutes from where I was living. If that had materialized into permanent, tenure-track employment, I would have probably worked on the history of antislavery.

I do think there are lessons from the past: political lessons and military lessons as well. I'm struck by the fact, for example, that Jefferson wrote a letter to John Adams in 1813 stating that all through history, in every society at every time, one party existed that favored the many while another party existed that favored the few, and political battles tended to revolve around that struggle between the many and the few. And that's how I see American politics. I see that struggle going on in the Revolution. I see that struggle going on between the Federalists and the Democratic Republican Party in the 1790s and the early days of the republic. I see it through most of the nineteenth and twentieth centuries in America's political history as well.

LUCAS: Are there other important lessons from the era of the American Revolution and the early republic?

FERLING: I think there are. The American Revolution, for example, can tell us a great deal about the limits of military power. Look at the relative strength of Great Britain and the colonies in 1775—it seemed as if there was no way that the colonists could win that war and that they were mad to go to war. And yet they wound up winning it. There were limits to British military power. In Vietnam the United States wound up making some of the same mistakes that the British had made in the 1770s, thinking they could do whatever they wished. I hope we haven't made that same mistake again with our recent policies.

The American Revolution says something about the cost of imperial power as well. The British found themselves caught up in four intercolonial wars between 1689 and the end of the French and Indian War in 1763, and they were driven deeply in debt as a result. They tried to extricate themselves from their indebtedness with policies that brought on the Anglo-American crisis and war.

I'm struck by the fact, too, in reading Gordon Wood's *Radicalism of the American Revolution* and Joyce Appleby's *Inheriting the Revolution* that both of those historians develop the idea of how different America had become by 1826. Almost no one could have dreamed in 1776 of how the Revolution would play out and the changes that it would bring. I'm not sure I agree entirely with Professor Wood, who argues that people such as Jefferson were ultimately disenchanted by what happened. I wouldn't go that far. But it reinforces the lesson that you just never know what's going to happen in history. You undertake something, and you think you know where you're going, but it always leads to things you can't foresee. In my survey classes I emphasize how World War II was a crucial factor in bringing on the modern civil rights revolution in the 1950s and 1960s and may have had a hand in bringing on the women's liberation movement in the 1960s and 1970s—certainly no one foresaw these developments when the U.S. went into war.

In the 1790s one of the things that really fascinates me is how George Washington and John Adams coped with great crises. In 1794 there was a hue and cry to go to war with Great Britain, and instead of going to war Washington opted to seek peace. He sent John Jay to London and eventually accepted a treaty that had many shortcomings. But the great virtue of the treaty was that it prevented a war that Washington thought would have been disastrous for the union. By the same token, Adams's entire presidency was taken up by the Quasi-War crisis with France. He was under enormous pressure, especially from the right wing of his party, to take a bellicose policy. He, too, resisted that and sought peace, even though he knew that his actions might wreck his chances for reelection in 1800. I think that both presidents ultimately acted more like statesmen than as politicians. There is a lesson there for subsequent leaders. What seems to be the best thing to do from a political standpoint may not be the best thing to do in the long-term interests of the nation or the historical reputation of the leader.

LUCAS: Your first book was a study of Joseph Galloway, a Loyalist, and his ideas. Yet the several books you wrote after that work have focused primarily on Revolutionary leaders. Why the shift? How did your initial work on Loyalism during the Revolution inform your subsequent work on the revolutionaries themselves?

FERLING: When I was starting out, actually still working on my master's degree, I found myself fascinated with dissenters. I was interested in the Copperheads in the Civil War and Loyalists in the Revolution. When I decided to specialize in the American Revolution era, I focused on the Loyalists. By the time I got to Joseph Galloway, it was 1969, and I was active in the antiwar protests. Galloway was a protester. It was a very different kind of thing; he was a conservative protester, and the antiwar protests I participated in were at the opposite end of the spectrum.

As I worked on Galloway, I found myself drawn to areas that I hadn't imagined I would go into—I tell my graduate students that this is a benefit of doing biography. Galloway was speaker of the house of the Pennsylvania

Assembly for about twenty years, so I had to learn a good bit about Pennsylvania politics. His political ally was Benjamin Franklin, and so I had to learn something him. And then during the war, after proclaiming his neutrality initially, Galloway opportunistically joined the British when he thought they were about to win the war in 1776. The British used him as a military intelligence official, and so I had to learn something about military history. When I came along—and it may still be like this in graduate school today—if you were taking a course on the American Revolution, the professor would usually just skip over all of the military aspects and say, "We'll leave that to armchair generals." So I hadn't really learned anything about military history in school. Further, Galloway wrote about twenty-five pamphlets or so during the Revolution, and I had to understand something about the ideology of the Revolution in order to sort out what Galloway was saying in contrast to what the Whigs were saying.

More than anything, however, working on Galloway peaked my interest in military history. When I finished the Galloway book, I decided to do a book on colonial warfare. I was particularly influenced at that time by Richard Kohn's "The Social History of the American Soldier" [*American Historical Review* 86 (1981): 553–67]. Kohn talked about a new military history, and it was new in the sense that military historians now were trying to look not only at how war affected society but also at how society affected war. The book that I wrote was called *A Wilderness of Miseries*. As I researched that book, I grew interested in George Washington. At that time no one had done a one-volume biography of Washington for about fifty years. Because we did have source materials here, at that time it was the Fitzpatrick edition of Washington's writings, I was able to do a biography of Washington and still later a biography of Adams. I was probably able to do about 95 percent of my research for both books here in Carrollton, Georgia—getting books and microfilm on interlibrary loan and using the modern editorial versions of my subjects' papers. So it was a matter both of interest and expediency.

LUCAS: What inspired you to become a historian, writer, and biographer?

FERLING: When I was an undergraduate, I had to take two courses in American history during my freshman year and two in Western Civ in my sophomore year, but neither turned me on to history. They were mostly just memorization courses, and I didn't like them. I had had some interest in history before I started college, but those courses pretty much turned me off. I got to the last semester of my sophomore year, and I had to declare a major. Fortunately for me, the guy who was teaching Western Civ fell ill and had to go in the hospital. In the time-honored tradition of academe, the low man on the totem pole in the history department got rushed in to teach the remainder of the course. He was a young historian right out of graduate school named William Painter, and he threw out the original syllabus. He had us read several paperbacks. I don't remember all of them, but one of them was Marcus Cunliffe's *George Washington: Man and Monument*. I remember being completely fascinated. Instead of listening to lectures, we read and discussed the books. I found myself really getting turned on and going to the library and wanting to read more about Washington. One of the other books was Alan Bullock's *Hitler: A Study in Tyranny*. So at least two of the books were biographies. That may well be the source of my interest in biography.

But there was also something else that was crucial. In the 1960s during the student protests, many of the schools began to abandon the requirement that students had to take both halves of Western Civ and both halves of U.S. history. They went over to a cafeteria approach, and you had to take a set number of courses in social science. And you could take history, or you could elect not to take any history at all. One of the things that historians quickly discovered was that if the students were given a choice, they wouldn't take history.

This aroused concern in the profession, and I remember reading a couple of presidential addresses delivered to historical associations. The thrust of these was to encourage historians to write narrative history, to try to write something that could reach the general public. That really resonated with me. I wanted to reach out to the general public as well. I felt that writing biographies would be a way to do that. And all through my career, in fact, I've tried not only to publish in scholarly journals but also to write articles for popular magazines, such as *American History* and the *Smithsonian Magazine*, as a way of reaching out to the general public.

One of the things that disturbs me today about the profession is that almost everything that's being done is in social history, and it doesn't appear that very much of that is being read by the general public. There have been some academic historians who have been able to reach the general public. Joseph Ellis and David Hackett Fischer come to mind. But they are not writing social history, they are writing political or military history. I wish more professional historians could succeed in reaching the general public as popular writers, such as David McCullough and Walter Isaacson, have succeeded in doing. Their success suggests to me that the general public is interested primarily in biography and political history.

LUCAS: Did you have literary ambitions prior to becoming a historian?

FERLING: When I was an undergraduate, I had no idea what I was going to do. My dad worked for a large chemical company, but he didn't have much of a formal education. He had the misfortune of graduating from high school just as the stock market crashed in 1929, so he wasn't able to go forward with college. He worked for Union Carbide where he was surrounded by engineers, and he very badly wanted me to be an engineer. But I didn't have the inclination and certainly didn't have the talent in math for that.

What I really wanted to do was be a sportswriter. I worked on the newspaper in high school and wrote some sports for that. One of the things that got me interested in history was a movie I saw in high school I've seen it since, and it's pretty awful, but at the age of sixteen I thought it was wonderful. It was a documentary called *The Twisted Cross* on the rise and fall of Hitler. That sent me to the library, and I started reading some things on history. And a lot of what I read was written by popular writers. I remember being very much taken by William L. Shirer's *Rise and Fall of the Third Reich,* which I read when I was an undergraduate. And I remember thinking that I would like to do something like that. And when I took that Western Civ course with Professor Painter, I went to his office and said, "How do you get to do something like this? Do you have to be wealthy, a man of means, to write these things?" His response was something like, "Hell no. You teach history in college." And I knew at that point what I wanted to do.

LUCAS: Two of your contemporaries, Bernard Bailyn and Gordon Wood, have focused on the ideas that they believe shaped America in the late eighteenth and early nineteenth century. An earlier generation of historians, the one that included Charles Beard, stressed the role of economic interest as an agent of historical change. Where do you stand?

FERLING: Actually, I straddle the fence, although I lean more toward the idea of economics playing the principal role in determining what happens in history. I certainly don't think ideas are unimportant. Look, for example, at abolitionism in the nineteenth century: many people wound up in the abolitionist movement because of Christianity and Christian thought—the notion that I am my brother's keeper. At the opposite end of the spectrum, in the twentieth century, racist ideas helped create Nazis. But by and large I tend to see economics as the determining role in history. I look at the Constitutional Convention, for example, and if I had to put my money on why the Constitution wound up being written as the founders wrote it, it would be more because of economics than ideology. I wouldn't rule out ideology. The founders certainly had read extensively in the political science of their day and tried to structure government so that one branch didn't become more powerful than another. But by and large I see something like the Constitutional Convention as composed of delegates who represented the economic interests of their states. It's telling that the southerners who come to the Constitutional Convention almost to a man were interested in protecting slavery and devising a document that could protect slavery. Northerner delegates from urban areas who came were interested in furthering the commercial interests of New York or Philadelphia or Boston. So I tend to see economics as the driving force there and, for the most part, throughout history.

Bernard Bailyn's *Ideological Origins of the American Revolution* came out in 1967, and I started work on my dissertation on Galloway in 1969. I was really very much influenced by Bailyn. His book threw open a window to me that had been closed. Most of my work to that point had been involved with looking at what Progressive historians had written in the 1920s and 1930s. They were dismissive of ideas, which they saw as tools that leaders used for propaganda purposes. Bailyn obviously took ideas extremely seriously, and he saw ideas as shaping action. I was very much taken with Bailyn and still frequently use *Ideological Origins* as a required text in my American Revolution class. More than any other book, it shaped the way I approached Galloway. But now, I have come full circle. To tell you the truth, if I was to go back and write another book on Galloway today, I would probably see him as tied to Philadelphia's mercantile community and its fear of change for economic reasons and develop that concept far more than I did thirty years ago.

LUCAS: Your book *A Leap in the Dark: The Struggle to Create the American Republic* appeared in the summer of 2003. What is the theme of the book?

FERLING: *A Leap in the Dark* looks at the era of the American Revolution, the half century between the Albany Conference in 1754 and Jefferson's inauguration as president in 1801. In the first half of the study, I am concerned with explaining why the Revolution occurred. I emphasize economic factors and the personal opportunities that many sensed would result from independence. Workers and some merchants, especially those in New England, came to see that breaking away from Britain's restrictive mercantile legislation was in their best interests. Similarly many who had invested—or hoped to invest—in land in the trans-Appalachian West came to see that they would be better off if Americans called the shots with regard to opening that vast region. In addition, many ambitious colonists despaired of accomplishing what they believed they were capable of achieving because of the limitations imposed by what Jefferson referred to as their "colonial subservience." Many years after the Revolution, John Adams wrote that all he had been able to hope for as a British colonist was to be a militia officer, sit in the colonial assembly, and achieve a comfortable standard of living. That was insufficient for him and for many others.

In the second half of the book, I look at what the Revolution meant to that generation. Until 1776 the focus of the protest was entirely on resisting British policy. Other than Tories, few appeared to think about what post-independence America would be like, and most who gave it some thought shrank from divulging their thoughts publicly. Then in 1776 Thomas Paine spoke of independence as the birthday of a new world and an opportunity to begin the world anew. I believe that he captured what some had been quietly thinking, while others, who were stirred by the Declaration of Independence, began to envision change after 1776. Of course, the most-conservative revolutionaries never imagined radical social and political change, and many were appalled by the changes that occurred during the last years of the war and the first years of peace. This portion of the book deals with how these two sides coalesced and the struggle that they waged between the end of the war in 1783 and the election of 1800. In many ways, it is a return to the Progressive interpretation, but I think I am more charitable than they were to the Federalists. The nationalists, or consolidationists, not only harbored legitimate concerns about national security, but through Hamiltonianism they created a modern and diversified economy.

LUCAS: What do you make of the recent and current scholarship that looks favorably and seriously at post-1760 British policy in North America? It strikes me that there's a feeling in the air among a lot of historians of early America that the continuation of the British Empire might not have been such a bad thing, maybe in some ways even preferable to American independence, especially with regard to slavery and the fate of American Indians.

FERLING: I don't agree with that. I see the Revolution as a great, liberating moment. I see it in Jeffersonian terms, and I see the election of 1800 as a revolution of 1800—a revolution in the sense that it made possible the fulfillment of the ideas that people like Thomas Paine had given voice to and that I think many Americans embraced. Paine talks about the Revolution as a chance to start the world anew. It's the first day of a new world, he says in *Common Sense*. And I think a great many Americans came to see that as the case. I think what makes the American Revolution at once frustrating and really interesting is that all of the focus—until you get into the war in 1775 and 1776—is on resisting British policy, and it's unlike any other modern revolution. There's no sense of domestic change by and large in that time period. And it's only when they start thinking seriously in 1775 and 1776 of declaring independence that some people like Paine do begin talking openly about change. The Americans fielded a citizens' army basically, and a lot of those people come out of the war thinking that "we want to make some really seminal changes here; this is going to be the payback for all of the sacrifice that we've gone through" or that they're sacrificing in order to make those changes. If the crisis had been resolved peacefully, and Britain had been in control, maybe eventually, toward the end of the nineteenth century as happened in England, there would have been a broadening of suffrage rights and whatever. But enormous change was unleashed, particularly, as Joyce Appleby makes clear in *Inheriting the Revolution,* between 1800 and the fiftieth anniversary of independence in 1826. The window was thrown open, and the possibility for change was brought about with Jefferson's victory in 1800.

LUCAS: Is liberation the theme of your book *Adams vs. Jefferson: The Election of 1800?*

FERLING: It has two themes. One is that eighteenth-century politics and politicians were decidedly modern. There were differences between the politics of the 1790s and the early twenty-first century, but what I found most striking was how many similarities existed. The parties were better organized by 1800 than I had expected them to be. They already employed what we now call "negative campaigning": they adroitly used the technology at their disposal to get out their message; they utilized every conceivable artifice to out-hustle their adversaries; and the presidential candidates, including President Adams, were actively involved—though in a surreptitious manner—in the presidential campaign.

The second theme is that the election of 1800 resulted in a "revolution of 1800." At first blush, the results of the election appear to be extremely close. There was little difference in the electoral totals between the two parties, and in the states where I was able to flesh out the voting results, the parties more often than not were rather evenly balanced. Yet I also found evidence of significant change. In the congressional elections as a whole, there were striking signs that the Federalists had been repudiated. In part, that was payback for their high taxes, the Alien and Sedition Acts, and what many believed had been a contrived war scare with France. But it also represented the hope of many that the promise of truly sweeping change that Thomas Paine and Thomas Jefferson had enunciated in 1776—change that would bring an end forever to many of the social and political limitations that had existed in colonial Anglo-America before 1776—would at long last be fulfilled.

LUCAS: I'm struck by the way you evoke the rhythms of daily life in the early nineteenth-century U.S. in your biography of John Adams. Have you learned a lot from the works of social and cultural history written by your Americanist colleagues, or did you get that from the Adams papers?

FERLING: Well, I think it was from both. I've always been interested in social history. In fact for many years as part of my regular teaching load, I taught two courses in social history, U.S. social history to and since the Civil War. And I've always incorporated a great deal of social history in my survey classes. I teach two survey courses and one upper-level course every semester. My two survey courses are mostly social history courses, and I probably incorporate far more than my students would like about farm life. I am really intrigued by farm life because I grew up in a more urban environment around Houston. But my mother was the daughter of a farmer who lived not too far from Pittsburgh, and we used to go back up there on vacations every summer. So I'd spend several days on my grandfather's farm, and I suppose it led me to become intrigued with what life was like for those who had lived on farms in earlier generations. My dad was a blue-collar worker, a hardhat, so I was also interested in the industrial workplace and have stressed that as well in my classes. Most of my outside readings in the survey courses were on things like birthing practices or marriage habits or diets or medicine and longevity and that sort of thing. So I have always been interested in social history. But I do think one of the problems with social history is trying to tie things together into a bigger, meaningful whole. I think with political history you can, for example, develop a theme around the growth of capitalism or the growth of democracy. But if you're dealing with what life was like for coalminers or mill hands, it's fascinating, and I think you want to try to understand how our ancestors lived, but I have some difficulty in tying it all together in something that's really meaningful. I can do that better from a political angle.

Political history broadens your understanding of the general time period that you're working in, and I think that's one of its advantages. Biography is the same. As you mentioned, it does force you—if you're looking at John Adams, for example—not only to look at the political side but also to try to come to grips with his private life. What was it like to be a lawyer in mid-eighteenth-century Massachusetts? What was family life like? What was he like as a parent? What kind of houses did he live in? What books did he read, and why? How did he travel?

LUCAS: You've spent a lot of time with the founders, particularly Adams, Jefferson, and Washington. How do you assess their respective personalities?

FERLING: Jefferson is a great contradiction. He's a racist, and you would want more from a guy who appears to be so enlightened. He's a slave owner, and unlike Washington who liberates his slaves in his will, Jefferson only liberates a handful of slaves. And they're all from the Hemings family. People find that side of Jefferson distasteful. But on the other side, here's this guy who sees the danger posed by the route that the Federalists are taking. He takes the lead in resisting the Alien and Sedition Acts, and more than any other person, he was responsible, starting about 1790, for piecing together a movement to oppose Hamiltonianism. Ultimately the nineteenth century, as it unfolded politically at any rate, was Jefferson's century. So there's a real dichotomy there in looking at Jefferson, and it makes him extremely fascinating.

I think almost everybody who looks at Washington comes away with pretty positive ideas. People look at Washington trying to find evidence of corruption on his part and just can't find it. He doesn't misuse power. He's not a great general, but he's not a bad general either. And I think the country was extremely fortunate to have Washington as its first president. I don't agree with everything that he did. As I said, I'm probably more of a Jeffersonian, and Washington wound up leaning clearly toward the Federalists in his presidency. But I do think that the country was fortunate to have him. When he was faced with that crisis with Great Britain in 1794, he didn't opt for war; he opted for peace. I think that if he'd opted for war, there is a real possibility that the United States wouldn't have survived that early period. The country was so divided between Anglophiles and Francophiles that it might have been pulled completely apart if it had been a long, tough war. He did have a kind of Olympian manner about him. He was an unapproachable individual. He doesn't appear to be a very warm person at all. I've often thought, for example, that if somehow or other I could spend an evening—go to dinner and have a couple of drinks—with one of these people, who would I probably prefer it to be? And certainly Washington would be the one I would be least interested in spending an evening with because he was so unapproachable. I'd probably opt for John Adams. If nothing else, he'd probably gossip, and I'd probably learn more from him than the others.

LUCAS: You've been extraordinarily prolific throughout your career, even while teaching three courses per semester. I wonder about your work habits. Do you write daily?

FERLING: Actually, the three courses a semester are about one-third of what I taught for more than my first twenty years at West Georgia. We were on a quarter system, and we taught three courses a quarter. So I taught nine courses a year, and we met each class five days a week. So I was in the classroom for three hours every day. In some respects, maybe that was good, because it disciplined me to come to work five days a week. Most of my colleagues currently teach a two-day-a-week schedule, but I still opt to teach a five-day-a-week schedule, so that I come up to the office every single day. All through my career, I have tried to work out a teaching schedule with a long block of time in order to write. And it's meant doing some things that I didn't particularly want to do. I taught an awful lot of night classes when we were teaching the three courses a quarter. Now I teach my classes in the afternoon, and I come to work at 8:00 A.M. and try to work in the library for up to four hours. I don't look at a stopwatch or anything, and on days when I'm just spinning my wheels, I pack it up and wait for a better day tomorrow. But generally I try to go to the library and work there for several hours every day, five days a week.

LUCAS: So that's where you do your writing as well as your research—in the library?

FERLING: Right, in the library. But then I come back, and, of course, I have the computer in my office. But I still compose in longhand. When I started my career, I worked with a typewriter, and I wasn't a good-enough typist to think about typing and think about writing simultaneously. So I got in the habit of writing in longhand, and I still do that. After I revise what I write in longhand, then I come back and put it on the computer and do all of my revisions. I once had an office mate who used to say that he loved research, but he hated writing. He thought that writing was just an exercise and sort of a necessary evil. I always saw writing as an art form and loved writing every bit as much as doing the research. I spend at least 50 percent of the time that goes into every book writing and rewriting and rewriting.

LUCAS: What do you have in the works now [2004], after the *Adams vs. Jefferson* book?

FERLING: Well, Oxford is going to publish that book some time in late September or early October. Since submitting the manuscript for the election-of-1800 book, I've begun working on a book on the War of Independence. I've always veered between biography or political history and military history. One of the writers I most admire is John Keegan, the British military historian. I absolutely loved his single-volume histories of World War I and World War II, which I think are useful for both a scholarly audience and a popular audience, and I'm writing a book on the War of Independence that is modeled on Keegan's template.

A World of Kings

Brendan McConville

In November 5, 1764, diarist John Rowe recorded that "a sorrowful accident" had happened in Boston's North End. A giant "carriage" constructed by the neighborhood's residents, carrying effigies of the Pope and other figures, had "run over a Boy's head" during a raucous procession "& he died instantly." In response to the tragedy, the authorities dismantled the effigies and sought to destroy a similar cart in the South End, the "North & South end Popes" as they were known. However, when the magistrates "went to the So. End [they] could not Conquer upon which the South End people brought out their pope & went in Triumph to the Northward" to seek victory in the traditional battle between the neighborhoods that occurred on Boston Common every November fifth. "At the Mill Bridge," Rowe continued, "a Battle begun," the North End people "having repaired their pope." Neighborhood pride was on the line—the North End traditionally prevailed in these battles—but on this day a repaired pope would not do, and "the South End people got the Battle . . . Brought away the North End pope & burnt Both of them at the Gallows . . . Several thousand people following them" to see the spectacle on Boston Neck. So ended the annual celebration of the foiling of Guy Fawkes's 1605 plot against King James I and the English nation.[1]

Certain images predominate in popular imagination when we think of colonial America. Somber Puritans, heads bowed in prayer when not hunting witches at Salem; broad-hatted Quakers preaching peace in the city of brotherly love; yeoman farmers chopping wood and tending crops; dignified Indian chiefs negotiating with the ever-increasing number of white settlers; Virginia tobacco planters living in Georgian mansions on the Northern Neck, served by African slaves; and deerskin-clad frontiersmen opening new lands and fighting against the various Indian nations. Scholars have refined

From *Historically Speaking* 8 (May/June 2007)

these images and added new ones to their more specific conversations: visions of midwives and wenches, merchant entrepreneurs, aggressive artisans, confidence men, enlightened intellectuals reading Country-influenced pamphlets, and evangelical preachers seeking to save souls from eternal hellfire. But mobile papist archetypes crushing innocent children, followed by nighttime battles on Boston Common? This all seems to be somehow foreign, un-American, at best the manifestation of lower-class rowdiness in a busy colonial port, at worst an early display of irrational religious bigotry.

Yet it was none of these things. Boston's North and South End gangs were remembering Pope's Day, one of a number of annual royal rites at the core of political life in an imperial America that existed before 1776. In that lost world, public holidays did not celebrate exceptionalism and democracy but rather expressed intense pride in Britain's kings and rejoiced in the empire's victories in the continuous struggle against Catholicism. The political culture's central focus was a physically distant but emotionally available Protestant British monarch who had the provincial population's impassioned loyalty.

This all-encompassing royal America has been gradually wiped from our national memory. Royalism, it has seemed to the general public and most American scholars, had never really taken deep root in colonial society. The provinces' social diversity and truncated (by European standards) social structures supposedly inhibited faith in king and country and paved the way somehow for a republican America. But was this really the case?

To answer this question takes a seemingly impossible leap of faith, for it requires us to forget the American Revolution. We are still, despite the best efforts of historical writers, so conditioned by the overwhelming power of the democratic reality created in the last two hundred–plus years that we can only imagine American history as some variant on that omnipresent world view. Despite decades of proclaimed hostility to "whiggish" and teleological history, most historians still treat the years between 1688 and 1776 as somehow a long prologue to the revolutionary crisis or American society's broader modernization. There are at least three identifiable strains in this historiography: one with the imperative to explain the emergence of American national character and democratic government, another that examines the roots of American capitalism, and, more recently, a host of studies seeking the origins of America's racial attitudes.

The historians who subscribe to these approaches believe that major changes develop over time and that looking for their early manifestations will tell us much about them. This idea has persistent emotional appeal: it is forward-looking, modernizing, and in the American context, democratizing. One thing leads to another; things that look alike tend to be related. Thus the provincial world has been filled with protorepublicans, readers of Country pamphlets, rising assemblies, plain-folk Protestants, budding contract theorists, protocapitalists, protoproletariat, protoliberals, modernizers—in short, future Americans.[2]

Like most scholars of my generation, I accepted these premises. A democratization or republicanization of politics marked by rising assemblies, economic expansion, liberalization, and new egalitarian evangelical Protestant religious movements were the dominant trends in provincial life that explained change. Monarchical allegiance was superficial, social stratification became a problem, and patriarchy as a social and political principle was eroding. Belief that some form of modernization drove change in colonial America still dominated the historiography of the period, and I endorsed its logic.

In time, I came to see provincial political culture and the first British Empire very differently from how it had been presented to me. To accept the received wisdom about the period silenced most of its voices and misrepresented those we do hear. Progress toward a republic and a liberal capitalist society, toward the America we know, had been read back through the Revolution's distorting lenses into a very different time with its own political-cultural-social dynamic.

In the royal America that existed between the Glorious Revolution and 1776, that which we call political culture, the milieu in which politics takes place, was decidedly monarchical and imperial, Protestant and virulently anti-Catholic, almost to the moment of American independence. The Anglicization of colonial governments and legal procedures was linked to the establishment of a calendar of officially orchestrated annual celebrations of Britain's Protestant rulers, their families, and the historic triumph of Protestantism over Catholicism. These rites expressed an ecumenical Protestant political culture whose values and symbols bound a transatlantic empire.

Writers who lived in this society internalized and reinforced its values. Almost everything printed between 1689 and 1775 expressed an intense admiration for the monarchy and situated it within a dynastic British history that ran back to the Anglo-Saxons, as well as in terms of the historic and ongoing struggle between Pan-European Protestantism and Catholicism, absolutism, and popery. Shaped by what they saw, heard, and read, an ever-growing number of provincials identified themselves as Britons and referenced versions of British and English history as their own. A flood of goods from the home islands encouraged these provincial Britons to affect English manners and consumption patterns. The Hanoverian dynasty became the purveyor of good taste. For seven decades, without hesitation or hypocrisy, provincials proclaimed their love of Britain's Protestant monarchs and loathing for the kings' enemies, particularly papists of all stripes.

Modern notions of secular and sacred life as distinctive are of little help in understanding such a society. Religious devotion and denominational allegiances were loaded with political implications. Politics was intertwined with religion and religious identity on all levels of society, as all British Americans somehow knew. By addressing religious developments apart from the political culture they occurred in, we have unintentionally distorted the character of early American politics.

The saturation of royal rites, the embrace of the Hanoverian monarchy, and the heightened dread of Catholics encouraged a particular matrix of emotions, expressed in print and in conversation, which described and mediated all power and personal relationships in the society. Love, fear, and desire, these passions of empire, became common tropes in decrees, official correspondence, and newspaper writings. They linked the colonies to London, and colonists to their monarch, giving a human structure to the allegiance to a place and a government never seen by most colonials. That love of the monarchy seemed only to intensify over time, spurred by imperial wars in which the colonists were centrally involved (especially the Seven Years' War) and the increasing commercial contacts between Britain and its western colonies.

Accepting the reality of this royal America, with its jumble of monarchical rites and royally focused affections, brings into sharp relief a historically unrecognizable British Empire and a pattern of change distinctive from the whiggish teleologies that dominate our understanding of the period. In some respects, the empire's political culture was the exact opposite of what has been commonly assumed.

In the home islands, the Glorious Revolution's constitutional settlement located sovereignty in the King-in-Parliament and more or less settled the balance of power in the government. Effectively this situated authority in the House of Commons and the imperial bureaucracy. People tried to forget the violent seventeenth century, when English society was rendered by civil war and revolution. The occasional Stuart conspiracy unsettled the national peace after 1689, but these were sporadic, ill planned, and tainted by the deposed house's French and Catholic connections. Political patronage, the Church of England's control of religious and social life in countless communities, fear of Europe's Catholic powers, and a fixed and controlled land-tenure system maintained allegiance to this government. It had to be so, as many eighteenth-century Englishman felt tepid at best toward their German-born Hanoverian kings, royal rites declined markedly in England, Jacobitism remained current in some circles, and republicanism took hold among coffeehouse radicals.

But American colonists came to understand the Glorious Revolution's legacy and the Hanoverian dynasty very differently. They saw the national settlement as establishing the Protestant succession and a Protestant political culture built around a cult of benevolent monarchy. Parliament had no symbolic role in imperial political rituals, its history was poorly understood, and it was diminished as a rhetorical presence in political discussions. For provincials, the monarch alone became the primary and common imperial link, the empire's living embodiment.

To accept this description of the colonists' views—and it is strongly supported by the print and manuscript sources—raises a series of questions that are not easy to reconcile with our received understanding of the colonial period, its primary trajectories of change, and the relationship of those transformations to the coming of the American Revolution. If the cult of Protestant monarchy was being inculcated and embraced, and political culture royalized and imperialized, how are we to explain the American Revolution?

The answer lies in considerable part within the political culture itself rather than in Enlightenment philosophy per se. The dramatic reorientation of the colonies' political culture after the Glorious Revolution was not tempered by the establishment of the social conventions or political structures that helped stabilize the social order in the home islands. State patronage remained extremely limited in the colonies, and the creation of new institutions was slow in relationship to population growth. The courts, the primary point of contact between the empire's authority and the mass of yeomen, were understood as a royal prerogative, and court procedures referenced all authority to the monarch. Provincial religious diversity stood in stark contrast to the church establishment of England itself. Freehold-land tenure was far more common in the colonies, and farmers violently resisted the efforts to establish tenancy as normal in parts of the countryside. However, these attributes did not make the colonists protorepublicans. Married to royal political spectacles and a slavishly loyal print culture, the result was a polity sown together by passions rather than patronage. British North Americans championed their British king with emotional intensity.

Divergent understandings of the king and the British constitution ultimately undid both the colonies' internal peace and the empire itself. As the political and social context changed after 1740, this (for lack of a better term) institutionally unconditioned royalism became latently subversive to the provincial order and ultimately to the entire empire. Explosive population growth, an expanding print culture, new ethnic and racial tensions, and warfare with the French and Native Americans encouraged some provincials to appropriate imperial rites and symbols during the conflicts such changes entailed. England's ambiguous, violent seventeenth-century history was used to justify all types of public behaviors. Rioting yeomen struggling for ownership of untold millions of acres in North America invoked a benevolent king to legitimate their violent actions, and rebelling slaves repeatedly claimed that the distant monarch intended to free them. Native Americans invoked Britain's king against his American subjects as more settlers moved into the interior. In incident after incident, colonists revealed that they loved the king. But they did not share a universal understanding of his nature, the character of political patriarchy, the British constitution, or even a perception of whether they lived under an imperial, British, English, or customary constitution.

This fragmentation helped tear the Anglo-American world apart. The failure to extend the British state's financial structures to America after the Seven Years' War grew as much from provincial society's royalization as it did from any other ideological factor. Affection for and faith in imagined kings and constitutions, coupled to unique understandings of British history, informed the colonists' actions in the imperial crisis as much as Country thought or natural-rights ideology did. Royal rites shaped the pattern of resistance in the streets as mobs confronted royal officials. The belief that the Glorious Revolution's settlement might manifest itself in their charters or in natural law informed colonial defiance of metropolitan norms. Only in 1774–75 did that royal America finally collapse amid a potent but decentralized terror against those loyal to the empire. An iconoclasm against royal emblems followed, punctuated by a series of symbolic regicides in the summer of 1776. In the terror's aftermath, the long struggle to make a workable republican society began.

Seen this way, colonial history becomes more than a preparation for the Revolution or the seed ground for the hyperdemocratic America we now live in. Rather, profoundly different assumptions shaped that world. By rejecting teleology, we let the colonists' lives speak to our own, not as agents of an emergent modernity but rather as human beings who inherited and adopted certain beliefs that they then used to confront change. By conceptualizing the period in this fashion, I am not claiming that provincials did not read "republican"- or "Country"-influenced tracts, that commerce did not expand dramatically, that election days and assemblies were not important, that religious revivals did not take place, or that no social oppression existed. But these changes occurred within the period's predominant political culture. Royalism was a primary force of change before 1776. What it was to be an American subject, in love with king and country, has been lost to us. But for the people of that time, it was a consuming attachment, one that separates their world from our own.

NOTES

1. John Rowe, diary, November 5, 1764, Massachusetts Historical Society, Boston.

2. The most sophisticated statement in this strain is Gordon S. Wood, *The Radicalism of the American Revolution* (New York: Knopf, 1991).

1816

A Year of Transition

C. Edward Skeen

Traditionally, at the close of every year, the media reviews the events of the past year and notes their significance—a form of "instant history." Contemporaries, however, are not necessarily good judges of the lasting consequences of developments so close to their experience. Often the importance of connections between little-noticed occurrences becomes evident only when seen from a distant period. Similarly historians trained to see sweeping developments from the myriad details that cover a decade or a century may just as easily miss the historical relevance of a small occurrence. Obviously a great deal of "event" history has been written encompassing a brief period, such as an election, a war, or even a battle, but events treated in thematic isolation tend to miss important clues that may derive a new collective meaning by focusing on a single year. A close study of that year (and not the event itself) may reveal valuable information about the context in which an event occurred. One-year histories offer yet another perspective and a different way to examine closely the synergy of events that make a period of history unique.

Books about a single year are nothing new; Bernard De Voto's work on 1846 comes to mind. Recently many historians have begun to focus a microscope on a single year. Books by Andrew Burstein (about the year 1826) and Louis P. Masur (about the year 1831) are two examples.[1] My study of the year 1816 adds to that list of works.[2] Admittedly, a case could be made that every year is unique and that the events of one year intertwine with strands from the past to weave the fabric of the future. It is obvious that some years are more unique than others, such as 1776 (Revolution), 1787 (Constitution),

1861 (Civil War), and so forth, that stand out in American memory because they mark developments that clearly have had a profound influence on the future course of American history. On the other hand, there are years that at first glance may not seem significant but may have witnessed events that in retrospect emerge as a significant turning point or a transition between two eras of American history.

There are many ways to approach the study of a year. Burstein, for example, used 1826 as a touchstone, relating biographically the contributions of unique individuals leading up to and after the year under study. Masur, on the other hand, chose to use broad thematic chapters to relate major movements evolving during 1831. My approach was to focus as closely as possible on the events of 1816 topically. Like Masur, I also tried to show how these events influenced future developments. As historians, we enjoy the luxury that contemporaries of that time did not—the ability to see how things turned out and to be able to assess how Americans of that day advanced the American republic and its people.

It might be asked why a year like 1816 would be chosen for a detailed study. A first impression suggests that 1816 could be labeled "A Year When Nothing Happened." This view arises, no doubt, from historians' dreadful neglect of the entire period between 1815 and 1825. These years, frequently labeled as the "Era of Good Feelings," are often given light and dismissive treatment as the writers of history textbooks seemingly rush to get to the more interesting post-1825 Jacksonian period. In truth, a lot happened in 1816. For example, 1816 was a critical year for making the decision to build the great Erie Canal. A study of the decision-making process is important for an understanding of the hopes and fears of New Yorkers as they considered this project. From the perspective of Americans of that time, it was a courageous step, fraught with great risk. From our perspective, it was a wise and farsighted venture that was successful far beyond their fondest hopes.

Interestingly, the most spectacular events of 1816 were things that most intrigued contemporaries of that time but in the final analysis were relatively inconsequential. The event that elicited the most comment from Americans in 1816 was the bizarre weather, known today as "The Year without a Summer." It snowed in New England in every month of that summer. Frost reached as far south as North Carolina and as far west as Indiana (that can be documented) in every month that summer. It was also extremely dry, and the combined effects of drought and crop-killing frosts naturally concerned not only farmers but also Americans in every walk of life. Ultimately this summer proved to be an anomaly brought on by the ejecta of a spectacular volcanic explosion in 1815 on the Indonesian island of Tambora. The weather soon returned to normal, and bountiful crops were harvested in 1817.

Another event that stirred the passions of Americans in 1816 and that had a more profound and prolonged effect was the public reaction to a congressional pay raise. The inflationary effects of the War of 1812 and the failure of banks south of New England to redeem their paper currency, supposedly backed by gold and silver, prompted congressmen who were receiving paper money redeemable at only about 75 percent of specie (gold and silver) to push through their first pay raise since the establishment of the government under the Constitution. Given the perceived hard times caused by the weather and by bank defaults, the pay raise seem inappropriate. Moreover, the mode of payment was altered from $6 a day to an annual salary of $1,500. The public reaction may have been generated at first by partisan politicians, but ultimately their response became a political tornado that swept approximately two-thirds of the sitting congressmen and senators out of office. Popular participation in protest meetings signaled a new phenomenon in politics, a decline in deference and a rise of popular democracy. While politicians had long ago learned how to pander to popular prejudice, it was the breadth of the response that amazed contemporary observers. As Joseph Gales, editor of the Washington, D.C., *Daily National Intelligencer,* noted, the Compensation Law protests "inspired those with eloquence who never spake before."[3] The chastisement delivered to the politicians of the Fourteenth Congress was a portent of the so-called "Rise of the Common Man." The power of the people was unleashed, and whether sincere or not, politicians thereafter had to pay due obeisance.

Perhaps the overriding feature of this year was the wave of nationalism that swept over the country. To a certain extent, this development was an outgrowth of the mixture of relief and joy felt by Americans after the War of 1812, which had bitterly divided the people politically but had ended on a high note—the victory of Andrew Jackson over the British at New Orleans. The celebration of the fortieth anniversary of American independence on the Fourth of July in 1816, the first full year of peace after the War of 1812, was marked by an unusual display of patriotism around the country. A common theme in the toasts and orations in 1816 was a call for unity—America's vast potential for greatness could only be achieved by coming together as one people.

A by-product of this feeling of general goodwill was an abatement of partisan politics. Members of the Fourteenth Congress frequently commented on the civility of the debates and the sense they had that partisan politics was on the wane. The phrase "Era of Good Feelings," so often maligned as inaccurate by historians, is in fact a fair characterization of the political situation in 1816. This was due largely to the advanced state of decline of the Federalist Party. This party was centered in New England, and Federalists had opposed the War of 1812 from its declaration. They continued to be harshly critical of the war, and three states, Massachusetts, Connecticut, and Rhode Island, refused to allow the government the use of their state militia during the war. Near the end of the war, Federalist leaders even called an antiwar meeting at Hartford, Connecticut, which resulted in proposals for Constitutional amendments. Unfortunately for them, their timing was atrocious, as the war ended before their demands could be presented to Congress. Now, in the aftermath of the war, their resistance seemed unpatriotic. They were so discredited that they did not even attempt to try to regroup and rebuild their party. In the election of 1816, the Federalists did not even field a presidential candidate. Rufus King, the putative nominee of the party, was in fact a candidate for governor of New York and never considered himself as the presidential nominee of his party.

Federalists undoubtedly feared political proscription and punishment for their opposition to the war, and they may have also feared isolation and a lack of government support for their section of the country. New England was at that time undergoing a metamorphosis. During the war, there was a growth of manufacturing, particularly in textiles. When the British emptied their warehouses in the aftermath of the war and flooded the American market with cheap manufactured goods, it hurt the fledgling industry. New Englanders particularly wanted protection in the form of tariffs, and they desperately hoped for repayment by the government for wartime expenses. Thus the goodwill of the government was a necessity.

Effectively, the Federalists sacrificed their party to mend their fences with the rest of the country. Conveniently the New England Federalists' efforts to play down partisan rancor coincided with the public's desire to heal the divisions created by the war and to reaffirm a common sentiment to advance their republican experiment. One result was a remarkable and productive legislative program advanced particularly by leaders, such as John C. Calhoun and Henry Clay. The legislative program bore a greater resemblance to the principles espoused by the Federalists than to those of the entrenched Republican Party. Federalists were pleased by the tolerance of the Republicans toward their old enemies, and they believed the Republican legislation vindicated their political tenets. They could hardly complain when the Republicans were enacting their programs, yet they also saw that they were being preempted. The Republicans were stealing the Federalist Party platform.

New Englanders were undoubtedly happy to secure the Tariff of 1816 that protected their manufactured goods. While there were sectional overtones during the debate, there was little to indicate the eventual political passions this issue evoked. The creation of the Second Bank of the United States restored stability to bank notes and made them redeemable at par with specie. National defense was improved by providing increased support for the training of military officers at the West Point Academy, the creation of a standing professional army, and increased appropriations to build up the United States Navy. Congress also passed a bill to create a fund for internal improvements (roads and canals), but this last bill was vetoed by President James Madison.

In addition to the remarkable political developments, 1816 was also notable for the development of organizations to advance humanitarian goals. If Americans were a nation of "joiners" by the 1830s, as Alexis de Tocqueville phrased it, that process began in 1816. No doubt, the growing spirit of American nationalism, as well as the ongoing effects of the Second Great Awakening, helped to foster the development of a number of societies to benefit humanity. There was also far more antislavery activity than has been heretofore noted by historians. The year ended with the formation of the American Colonization Society. Other humanitarian reforms that drew the attention of Americans in 1816 include a temperance movement, a peace movement, penal reform, the formation of the American Bible Society, a Sunday-school movement as well as other public educational reforms, and a Sabbatarian movement to stop the delivery of Sunday mail.

From many points of view, 1816 was indeed a year of transition. The American economy was on the threshold of an emerging market revolution, particularly with the development of textile manufacturing in New England and the beginnings of a transportation network epitomized by the Erie Canal. While the former gained only minimal support from the national government and the latter project none at all, both the national and state governments gave hints of positive support for the growth of the economy, and the establishment of the Second National Bank promised a sounder and more stable currency. Politically the demise of the Federalist Party portended the development of a new party system with a broader-based popular participation. Socially the development of many new voluntary associations in 1816 hinted not only of a growing community awareness but also a growing sense of nationhood.

NOTES

1. Bernard De Voto, *The Year of Decision, 1846* (Boston: Little, Brown, 1943); Andrew Burstein, *America's Jubilee: How in 1826 a Generation Remembered 50 Years*

of Independence (New York: Knopf, 2001); Louis P. Masur, *1831: Year of Eclipse* (New York: Hill and Wang, 2001). See also, for example, Stephen Saunders Webb, *1676: The End of American Independence* (Cambridge, Mass.: Harvard University Press, 1985), and Kenneth M. Stampp, *America in 1857: A Nation on the Brink* (New York: Oxford University Press, 1990).

2. C. Edward Skeen, *1816: America Rising* (Lexington: University Press of Kentucky, 2003).

3. *Daily National Intelligencer,* June 13, 1816.

Further Readings

The literature on early American history is vast. Any bibliography flirting with comprehensiveness would require a separate volume. The following list of suggested readings represents a sampling of some of the best and most innovative recent work along with some influential classic titles. It is intended merely to assist the reader to explore the richness of early American history. Any taxonomy of early American historiography runs into significant difficulties that in many ways mirror the robust messiness of the field itself. A strictly chronological scheme is not workable for those many books that pursue their subjects without regard for crossing the blurred and shifting boundaries between periods. And even for those books whose contents fall cleanly within one of the recognized periods of early American history, it is often not at all clear whether a given title is best listed by period or approach. The following list combines three chronological sections—Colonial, Revolution, and Early Republic—with a number of topical sections, including Atlantic World, Cultural and Social History, Founders, Historiography, Military and Naval History, and Religious History.

First Contacts/Colonial History

Anderson, Virginia DeJohn. *Creatures of Empire: How Domestic Animals Transformed Early America.* New York: Oxford University Press, 2004.

———. *New England's Generation: The Great Migration and the Formation of Society and Culture in the Seventeenth Century.* Cambridge, U.K.: Cambridge University Press, 1991.

Bremer, Francis J. *John Winthrop: America's Forgotten Founding Father.* New York: Oxford University Press, 2003.

Calloway, Colin G. *New Worlds for All: Indians, Europeans, and the Remaking of Early America.* Baltimore: Johns Hopkins University Press, 1997.

———. *The Scratch of Pen: 1763 and the Transformation of North America.* New York: Oxford University Press, 2006.

Cronon, William. *Changes in the Land: Indians, Colonists, and the Ecology of New England.* New York: Hill and Wang, 1983.

Crosby, Alfred W. *The Columbian Exchange: Biological and Cultural Consequences of 1492.* 1972. Westport, Conn.: Praeger, 2003.

Demos, John P. *Entertaining Satan: Witchcraft and the Culture of Early New England.* New York: Oxford University Press, 1982.

———. *A Little Commonwealth: Family Life in Plymouth Colony.* New York: Oxford University Press, 1970.

Donahue, Brian. *The Great Meadow: Farmers and the Land in Colonial Concord.* New Haven, Conn.: Yale University Press, 2004.

———. *Reclaiming the Commons: Community Farming and Forestry in a New England Town, New Haven.* New Haven, Conn.: Yale University Press, 1999.

Fischer, David Hackett. *Albion's Seed: Four British Folkways in America.* New York: Oxford University Press, 1989.

Gaustad, Edwin S. *Roger Williams.* New York: Oxford University Press, 2005.

Greene, Jack P. *Peripheries and Center: Constitutional Development in the Extended Polities of the British Empire and the United States, 1607–1788.* Athens: University of Georgia Press, 1986.

———. *Pursuits of Happiness: The Social Development of Early Modern British Colonies and the Formation of American Culture.* Chapel Hill: University of North Carolina Press, 1988.

Horn, James. *A Land as God Made It: Jamestown and the Birth of America.* New York: Basic Books, 2005.

Kidd, Thomas S. *The Protestant Interest: New England after Puritanism.* New Haven, Conn.: Yale University Press, 2004.

Kupperman, Karen Ordahl. *The Jamestown Project.* Cambridge, Mass.: Harvard University Press, 2007.

Lepore, Jill. *The Name of War: King Philip's War and the Origins of American Identity.* New York: Knopf, 1998.

Mancall, Peter C. *Hakluyt's Promise: An Elizabethan's Obsession for an English America.* New Haven, Conn.: Yale University Press, 2007.

McConville, Brendan. *The King's Three Faces: The Rise and Fall of Royal America.* Chapel Hill: Omohundro Institute of Early American History and Culture/ University of North Carolina Press, 2006.

Morgan, Edmund S. *American Slavery, American Freedom: The Ordeal of Colonial Virginia.* 1975. New York: Norton, 2003.

Norton, Mary Beth. *In the Devil's Snare: The Salem Witchcraft Crisis of 1692.* New York: Knopf, 2002.

Taylor, Alan. *American Colonies.* New York: Viking, 2001.

Wood, Peter H. *Strange New Land: Africans in Colonial America.* New York: Oxford University Press, 2002.

Revolution

Bailyn, Bernard. *The Ideological Origins of the American Revolution.* 1967. Cambridge, Mass.: Belknap, 1992.

Breen, T. H. *The Marketplace of Revolution: How Consumer Politics Shaped American Independence.* New York: Oxford University Press, 2004.

Butler, Jon. *Becoming America: The Revolution before 1776.* Cambridge, Mass.: Harvard University Press, 2000.

Carp, Benjamin L. *Rebels Rising: Cities and the American Revolution.* New York: Oxford University Press, 2007.

Ferling, John. *A Leap in the Dark: The Struggle to Create the American Republic.* New York: Oxford University, 2003.

———. *Almost a Miracle: The American Victory in the War of Independence.* New York: Oxford University Press, 2007.
Fischer, David Hackett. *Paul Revere's Ride.* New York: Oxford University Press, 1994.
———. *Washington's Crossing.* New York: Oxford University Press, 2004.
Foner, Eric. *Tom Paine and Revolutionary America.* 1976. New York: Oxford University Press, 1997.
Gross, Robert A. *The Minutemen and Their World.* 1976. New York: Hill and Wang, 2001.
Maier, Pauline. *American Scripture: Making the Declaration of Independence.* New York: Knopf, 1997.
———. *From Resistance to Revolution: Colonial Radicals and the Development of American Opposition to Britain, 1765–1776.* 1972. New York: Norton, 1991.
McDonald, Forrest. *Novus Ordo Seclorum: The Intellectual Origins of the Constitution.* Lawrence: University of Kansas Press, 1986.
Middlekauff, Robert. *The Glorious Cause: The American Revolution, 1763–1789.* Rev. ed. New York: Oxford University Press, 2007.
Nash, Gary B. *The Unknown American Revolution: The Unruly Birth of Democracy and the Struggle to Create America.* New York: Viking, 2005.
Norton, Mary Beth. *Liberty's Daughters: The Revolutionary Experience of American Women.* Boston: Little, Brown, 1980.
Wood, Gordon S. *The American Revolution: A History.* New York: Modern Library, 2002.
———. *The Creation of the American Republic, 1776–1787.* Chapel Hill: University of North Carolina Press, 1969.
———. *The Radicalism of the American Revolution.* New York: Knopf, 1991.

Early Republic

Appleby, Joyce. *Inheriting the Revolution: The First Generation of Americans.* Cambridge, Mass.: Harvard University Press, 2000.
Brands, W. H. *Andrew Jackson: His Life and Times.* New York: Doubleday, 2005.
Elkins, Stanley, and Eric McKitrick. *The Age of Federalism: The Early American Republic, 1788–1800.* New York: Oxford University Press, 1993.
Ferling, John. *Adams vs. Jefferson: The Tumultuous Election of 1800.* New York: Oxford University Press, 2004.
Fischer, David Hackett. *Liberty and Freedom: A Visual History of America's Founding Ideas.* New York: Oxford University Press, 2004.
Howe, Daniel Walker. *What Hath God Wrought: The Transformation of America, 1815–1848.* New York: Oxford University Press, 2007.
Kerber, Linda. *Women of the Republic: Intellect and Ideology in Revolutionary America.* Chapel Hill: University of North Carolina Press, 1980.
Kukla, John. *A Wilderness So Immense: The Louisiana Purchase and the Destiny of America.* New York: Knopf, 2003.
Newman, Simon. *Parades and the Politics of the Street: Festive Culture in the Early American Republic.* Philadelphia: University of Pennsylvania Press, 1997.

Norton, Mary Beth. *Founding Mothers and Fathers: Gendered Power and the Forming of American Society.* New York: Knopf, 1996.
Rakove, Jack N. *His Original Meanings: Politics and Ideas in the Making of the Constitution.* New York: Knopf, 1997.
Richards, Leonard. *Shays's Rebellion: The American Revolution's Final Battle.* Philadelphia: University of Pennsylvania Press, 2002.
Sellers, Charles. *The Market Revolution: Jacksonian America, 1815–1816.* New York Oxfvord University Press, 1991.
Skeen, C. Edward. *1816: America Rising.* Lexington: University of Kentucky Press, 2003.
Taylor, Alan. *William Cooper's Town: Power and Persuasion on the Frontier of the Early American Republic.* Chapel Hill: University of North Carolina Press, 1995.
Waldstreicher, David. *In the Midst of Perpetual Fetes: The Making of American Nationalism, 1776–1820.* Chapel Hill: University of North Carolina Press, 1997.
Wilentz, Sean. *The Rise of American Democracy: Jefferson to Lincoln.* New York: Norton, 2005.

Atlantic World

Armitage, David, and Michael J. Braddick. *The British Atlantic World, 1500–1800.* Basingstoke and New York: Palgrave Macmillan, 2002.
Bailyn, Bernard. *Atlantic History: Concept and Contours.* Cambridge, Mass.: Harvard University Press, 2005.
Carretta, Vincent. *Equiano the African: Biography of a Self-Made Man.* Athens: University of Georgia Press, 2005.
Davis, David Brion. *Inhuman Bondage: The Rise and Fall of Slavery in the New World.* New York: Oxford University Press, 2006.
Elliott, John H. *Empires of the Atlantic World: Britain and Spain in America, 1492–1830.* New Haven, Conn.: Yale University Press, 2007.
Eltis, David. "Atlantic History in Global Perspective." *Itinerario* 23 (1999): 141–61.

Cultural and Social History

Axtell, James. *Natives and Newcomers: The Cultural Origins of North America.* New York: Oxford University Press, 2000.
Berkin, Carol. *First Generations: Women in Colonial America.* New York: Hill and Wang, 1996.
Berlin, Ira. *Many Thousands Gone: The First Two Centuries of Slavery in North America.* Cambridge, Mass.: Harvard University Press, 1998.
Brown, Kathleen M. *Good Wives, Nasty Wenches, and Anxious Patriarchs: Gender, Race, and Power in Colonial Virginia.* Chapel Hill: University of North Carolina Press, 1996.
Bushman, Richard L. *From Puritan to Yankee: Character and the Social Order in Connecticut, 1690–1765.* Cambridge, Mass.: Harvard University Press, 1967.
———. *The Refinement of America: Persons, Houses, and Cities.* New York: Vintage, 1993.

Further Readings

Butler, Jon. *Becoming America: The Revolution before 1776.* Cambridge, Mass.: Harvard University Press, 2000.

Demos, John. *The Unredeemed Captive: A Family Story from Early America.* New York: Knopf, 1994.

Gray, Edward G. The *Making of John Ledyard.* New Haven, Conn.: Yale University Press, 2007.

———. *New World Babel: Languages and Nations in Early America.* Princeton, N.J.: Princeton University Press, 1999.

Greven, Philip. *Four Generations: Population, Land, and Family in Colonial Andover, Massachusetts.* Ithaca, N.Y.: Cornell University Press, 1970.

Isaac, Rhys. *The Transformation of Virginia.* Chapel Hill: University of North Carolina Press, 1982.

Lindman, Janet Moore, and Michelle Lise Tarter, eds. *A Centre of Wonders: The Body in Early America.* Ithaca, N.Y.: Cornell University Press, 2001.

Lockridge, Kenneth. *A New England Town: The First Hundred Years, Dedham, Massachusetts, 1636–1736.* New York: Norton, 1970.

McWilliams, James E. *Building the Bay Colony: Economy and Culture in Early Massachusetts.* Charlottesville: University of Virginia Press, 2007.

———. *A Revolution in Eating: How the Quest for Food Shaped America.* New York: Columbia University Press, 2005.

Nash, Gary B. *Red, White, and Black: The Peoples of Early North America.* 1974. 3rd ed. Englewood Cliffs, N.J.: Prentice Hall 1991.

Rath, Richard Cullen. *How Early America Sounded.* Ithaca, N.Y.: Cornell University Press, 2003.

Shoemaker, Nancy. *A Strange Likeness: Becoming Red and White in Eighteenth-Century North America.* New York: Oxford University Press, 2004.

———, ed. *Clearing a Path: Theorizing the Past in Native American Studies.* New York: Routledge, 2002.

Sidbury, James. *Becoming African in America: Race and Nation in the Early Black Atlantic, 1760–1830.* New York: Oxford University Press, 2007.

Silver, Peter. *Our Savage Neighbors: How Indian War Transformed Early America.* New York: Norton, 2007.

St. George, Robert Blair, ed. *Becoming Colonial in Early America.* Ithaca, N.Y.: Cornell University Press, 2000.

Ulrich, Laurel Thatcher. *A Midwife's Tale: The Life of Martha Ballard, Based on Her Diary, 1785–1812.* New York: Knopf, 1990.

White, Richard. *The Middle Ground: Indians, Empires, and Republics in the Great Lakes Region, 1650–1815.* Cambridge, U.K.: Cambridge University Press, 1991.

Zuckerman, Michael. *Peaceable Kingdoms: New England Towns in the Eighteenth Century.* New York: Random House, 1970.

Founders

Bolton, Terry. *Taming Democracy: "The People," the Founders, and the Troubled End of the American Revolution.* New York: Oxford University Press, 2007.

Brands, W. H. *The First American: The Life and Times of Benjamin Franklin*. New York: Doubleday, 2000.
Brookhiser, Richard. *Alexander Hamilton, American*. New York: Free Press, 1999.
———. *Gentleman Revolutionary: Gouverneur Morris, the Rake Who Wrote the Constitution*. New York: Free Press, 2003.
Ellis, Joseph J. *American Creation: Triumphs and Tragedies at the Founding of the Creation*. New York: Knopf, 2007.
———. *American Sphinx: The Character of Thomas Jefferson*. New York: Knopf, 1997.
———. *Founding Brothers*. New York: Vintage, 2000.
———. *His Excellency: George Washington*. New York: Knopf, 2004.
Ferling, John. *John Adams: A Life*. Knoxville, Tenn.: Henry Holt, 1992.
Higginbotham, Don. *George Washington: Uniting a Nation*. Lanham, Md.: Rowman and Littlefield, 2002.
Isaacson, Walter. *Benjamin Franklin: An American Life*. New York: Simon and Schuster, 2003.
McCullough, David. *John Adams*. New York: Simon and Schuster, 2001.
Onuf, Peter S. *The Mind of Thomas Jefferson*. Charlottesville: University of Virginia Press, 2007.
Wood, Gordon S. *The Americanization of Benjamin Franklin*. New York: Penguin, 2004.
———. *Revolutionary Characters: What Made the Founders Different*. New York: Penguin, 2006.

Historiography, Debates, and General Essays

Calloway, Colin G., and Neal Salisbury, eds. *Reinterpreting New England Indians and the Colonial Experience*. Boston: Colonial Society of Massachusetts/University of Virginia Press, 2003.
Kennedy, Michael V., and William G. Shade, eds. *The World Turned Upside Down: The State of Eighteenth-Century American Studies at the Beginning of the Twenty-First Century*. Bethlehem, Penn.: Lehigh University Press, 2001.
Palsey, Jeffrey L., Andrew W. Robertson, and David Waldstreicher, eds. *Beyond the Founders: New Approaches to the Political History of the Early American Republic*. Chapel Hill: University of North Carolina Press, 2004.
Taylor, Alan. *Writing Early American History*. Philadelphia: University of Pennsylvania Press, 2005.

Military and Naval History

Anderson, Fred. *Crucible of War: The Seven Years' War and the Fate of British North America, 1754–1766*. New York: Knopf, 2000.
Grenier, John. *The First Way of War: American War Making on the Frontier, 1607–1814*. Cambridge, U.K.: Cambridge University Press, 2005.
Higginbotham, Don. *The War of American Independence: Military Attitudes, Policies, and Practice, 1763–1789*. New York: Macmillan, 1971.
Shy, John. *A People Numerous and Armed: Reflections on the Military Struggle for American Independence*. Rev. ed. Ann Arbor: University of Michigan Press, 1990.

Steele, Ian K. *Warpaths: Invasions of North America, 1613–1765.* New York: Oxford University Press, 1994.
Tilley, John A. *The British Navy and the American Revolution.* Columbia: University of South Carolina Press, 1987.
Volo, James M. *Blue Water Patriots: The American Revolution Afloat.* Westport, Conn.: Praeger, 2000.

Religious History

Bonomi, Patricia U. *Under the Cope of Heaven: Religion, Society, and Politics in Colonial America.* 1986. New York: Oxford University Press, 2003.
Butler, Jon. *Awash in a Sea of Faith: Christianizing the American People.* Cambridge, Mass.: Harvard University Press, 1992.
Foster, Stephen. *The Long Argument: English Puritanism and the Shaping of New England Culture, 1570–1700.* Chapel Hill: University of North Carolina Press, 1991.
Hall, David D. *Worlds of Wonder, Days of Judgment: Popular Religious Belief in Early New England.* New York: Knopf, 1989.
Kidd, Thomas S. *Awakenings: The First Generation of American Evangelical Christianity.* New Haven, Conn.: Yale University Press, 2007.
Marsden, George M. *Jonathan Edwards: A Life.* New Haven, Conn.: Yale University Press, 2003.
Miller, Perry. *Errand into the Wilderness.* 1956. Cambridge, Mass.: Harvard University Press, 2000.
Noll, Mark. *America's God: From Jonathan Edwards to Abraham Lincoln.* New York: Oxford University Press, 2002.
Stout, Harry S. *The New England Soul: Preaching and Religious Culture in Colonial New England.* New York: Oxford University Press, 1986.

Contributors

JEREMY DUPERTUIS BANGS is director of the Leiden American Pilgrim Museum. He has written extensively on sixteenth- and seventeenth-century Dutch and colonial American history.

BRIAN DONAHUE is an associate professor of American Environmental Studies at Brandeis University. He is the author of *Reclaiming the Commons: Community Farming and Forestry in a New England Town, New Haven* (1999) and *The Great Meadow: Farmers and the Land in Colonial Concord* (2004).

JOHN FERLING is a professor emeritus of history at the University of West Georgia. He has written extensively on the political and military history of early America. His latest book is *Almost a Miracle: The American Victory in the War of Independence* (2007). Among his other books are *Setting the World Ablaze: Washington, Adams, Jefferson and the American Revolution* (2000); *A Leap in the Dark: The Struggle to Create the American Republic* (2003); and *Adams vs. Jefferson: The Tumultuous Election of 1800* (2004).

EDWARD G. GRAY is associate professor of history at Florida State University. He is author of *New World Babel: Languages and Nations in Early America* (1999) and The *Making of John Ledyard* (2007). He is editor of *Common-place*, an award-winning Web magazine devoted to early American history.

DON HIGGINBOTHAM is Dowd Professor of History at the University of North Carolina at Chapel Hill. His most recent book is *George Washington: Uniting a Nation* (2002).

J. DAVID HOEVELER is professor of history at the University of Wisconsin-Milwaukee and author of *Creating the American Mind: Intellect and Politics in the American Colonial Colleges* (2002).

JAMES HORN is vice president of research for the Colonial Williamsburg Foundation and Abby and George O'Neill Director of the John D. Rockefeller Jr. Library at Colonial Williamsburg. He is also a lecturer at the College of William and Mary. He is author of numerous books and articles on colonial America, including *A Land as God Made It: Jamestown and the Birth of America* (2005).

THOMAS S. KIDD is associate professor of history at Baylor University. He is author of *The Protestant Interest: New England after Puritanism* (2004), *The Great Awakening: The Roots of Evangelical Christianity in Colonial America* (2007), and *The Great*

Awakening: A Brief History with Documents (2007). He is also working on two new books: *American Christians and Islam* and *A Christian Sparta: Evangelicals, Deists, and the Creation of the American Republic.*

JOSEPH S. LUCAS is editor of *Historically Speaking* and assistant director of the Historical Society. His articles have appeared in *Explorations in Early American Culture* and *The Journal of the Historical Society.*

PAULINE MAIER is the William R. Kenan, Jr. Professor of American History at the Massachusetts Institute of Technology. Her *American Scripture: Making the Declaration of Independence* (1997) was a finalist in General Nonfiction for the National Book Critics' Circle Award. She is now writing a narrative history of the ratification of the federal Constitution.

PETER C. MANCALL is professor of history and anthropology at the University of Southern California and director of the USC-Huntington Early Modern Studies Institute. His most recent book is *Hakluyt's Promise: An Elizabethan's Obsession for an English America* (2007). He is the editor of *The Atlantic World and Virginia, 1550–1624* (2007) and is currently writing "Hudson's Fatal Journey," to be published by Basic Books in 2009.

BRENDAN MCCONVILLE is professor of history at Boston University. His most recent book is *The King's Three Faces: The Rise and Fall of Royal America* (2006). He is working on a book on the American Revolution.

JAMES E. MCWILLIAMS is associate professor of history at Texas State University–San Marcos. He is author of *A Revolution in Eating: How the Quest for Food Shaped America* (2005) and *Building the Bay Colony: Economy and Culture in Early Massachusetts* (University of Virginia Press, 2007).

PETER S. ONUF is the Thomas Jefferson Foundation Professor of History at the University of Virginia and in 2008–9 the Harmsworth Professor of American History at Oxford University. His most recent books are *The Mind of Thomas Jefferson* (2007) and *Nations, Markets, and War: Modern History and the American Civil War,* with Nicholas G. Onuf (2006).

PAUL A. RAHE is professor of history and political science at Hillsdale College. He is the author of *Republics Ancient and Modern: Classical Republicanism and the American Revolution* (1992) and *Against Throne and Altar: Machiavelli and Political Theory under the English Republic* (forthcoming, 2008).

JACK N. RAKOVE is William Robertson Coe Professor of History and American Studies and professor of political science and (by courtesy) of law at Stanford University. *His Original Meanings: Politics and Ideas in the Making of the Constitution* (1997) won the Pulitzer Prize in History.

C. EDWARD SKEEN is professor emeritus of history at the University of Memphis. He has written a number of books, including most recently *1816: America Rising* (2003).

RANDALL J. STEPHENS is assistant professor of history at Eastern Nazarene College. He is author of *The Fire Spreads: Holiness and Pentecostalism in the American South*

(2007). He is an editor of the *Journal of Southern Religion* and associate editor of *Historically Speaking*.

GORDON S. WOOD is Alva O. Way University Professor and Professor of History at Brown University. He is the author of many important books in early American history, including *The Creation of the American Republic, 1776–1787* (1969), which won the Bancroft Prize and the John H. Dunning Prize; *The Radicalism of the American Revolution* (1992), which won the Pulitzer Prize for History and the Ralph Waldo Emerson Prize; *The Americanization of Benjamin Franklin* (2004); and *Revolutionary Characters: What Made the Founders Different* (2006). He is currently working on a volume in the *Oxford History of the United States* dealing with the period of the early Republic from 1789 to 1815.

DONALD A. YERXA is assistant director of the Historical Society and professor of history at Eastern Nazarene College. He has been editor of *Historically Speaking* since 2001. He is the author of three books, including *Admirals and Empire* (1991), and editor of several volumes in the University of South Carolina Press series Historians in Conversation.

Index

A Is for American. See Lepore, Jill
Adams, John, 87, 89, 110–12, 115, 117–19
Adams, John Quincy, 62–63
Adams, Samuel, 37, 86–87
Albany Conference/Congress (1754), 101, 105, 115
Alden, John R., 24
Alienation and Sedition Acts, 117–18
Alison, Francis, 90
Allerton, Isaac, 66
American Colonies. See Taylor, Alan
American Colonization Society, 132
American exceptionalism, 10, 28–29, 122
American Revolution, 2–3, 10–16, 20–22, 25–27, 28–29, 33–34, 37–39, 41–42, 55, 86–90, 91–92, 94–95, 107, 110–12, 115–18, 122–23, 125–26, 128
American Scripture. See Maier, Pauline
Anderson, Benedict, 3, 5, 29
Andrews, Charles, 24
Anglican Church, 54, 68–69, 83–84, 90
Anne (queen of England), 69
Appleby, Joyce, 110, 117
Archive of Americana (Readex), 1
Articles of Confederation, 107
Ashe, Thomas, 96
Atlantic history, 11–12, 25–26, 31, 38, 40
Atlantic world, 2, 11–12, 20, 41, 71, 74

Backus, Isaac, 84
Bailyn, Bernard, 11, 24, 25, 33, 37–38, 40, 65, 114–15
Baltimore, 95
Bangs, Jeremy Dupertuis, 5. *See also* Pilgrims
Baptists, 84, 89–90
Beard, Charles, 114
Beeman, Richard, 27

Bellamy, Joseph, 87–88
Berkeley, George, 85
Berlin, Ira, 12
Bidwell, Percy, 73
Billington, James, 101
Blackstone, William, 89
Bodle, Wayne, 39
Bolton, Herbert Eugene, 26
Boorstin, Daniel, 25
Boston, 69–71, 86–87, 95, 103–4, 115, 121–22
Bradford, William, 60, 62, 66, 104
Breen, T. H., 25
British constitution, 89, 125–26
British Empire, 19–21, 25, 71, 116, 123–24
Brown, Richard D., 38
Buel, Richard, 39
Bullock, Alan, 113
Burstein, Andrew, 128–29
Butler, Jon, 42

Cabot, John and Sebastian, 47, 50
Calhoun, John C., 131
Canada, 16, 108
Caribbean, 16, 48
Catesby, Mark, 93
Catholicism, 5, 47, 51, 67–72, 122–23
Central America, 48
Certeau, Michel de, 3
Chaplin, Joyce, 10
Charles II (king of England), 68, 104
Charleston, 95
Chernow, Ron, 27
Chesapeake region, 9, 38, 54, 57–58, 94, 102–5
Chile, 26
Clap, Thomas, 85
Clarke, John, 104

Clay, Henry, 131
Coddington, William, 104
coherence of historical inquiry, 1–3, 77, 107
Coke, Sir Edward, 88
Collamore, Peter and Anthony, 66
College of New Jersey (Princeton), 83–84, 88–89
College of Philadelphia (University of Pennsylvania), 83, 85, 90
College of William and Mary, 83, 85–86, 88
Colley, Linda, 79
Colman, Benjamin, 69, 72
colonial colleges, 83–90
Columbian Exchange. *See* Crosby, Alfred
Columbus, Christopher, 47, 52
Common Sense. See Paine, Thomas
complexity in historical studies, 1–3, 26, 42, 50, 54
Concord, Mass., 5, 25, 73–82, 89
Connecticut, 68, 80, 84–85, 87, 103, 105, 131
Constitutional Convention (1787), 34, 41, 101, 114
Continental Congress, 18, 38, 89
contingency in historical studies, 7, 15, 59
Cooper, Myles, 88
Creation of the American Republic. See Wood, Gordon S.
Cromwell, Oliver, 68
Cronon, William, 74
Crosby, Alfred, 9
Cudworth, James, 65
Cunliffe, Marcus, 113
Cushing, John, 66

Daniell, Jere, 38
Darnton, Robert, 19
Dartmouth College, 83–85, 90
Declaration of Independence, 14, 30, 32, 89, 116
Deetz, James and Patricia Scott, 60–61, 65
Democratic Republican Party, 110
Dickens, Charles, 96
Documentary History of the Ratification of the Constitution, 13, 17
Doerflinger, Thomas, 40

Dominion of New England, 68
Donahue, Brian, 5. *See also* husbandry; Concord, Mass.
Dowd, Gregory Evans, 20
Dummer, Jeremiah, 85
Dunlap, William, 95
Dutch Reformed Church, 83–84
Dwight, Timothy, 73–74

East India Company (British), 51
Eccles, W. J., 26
Edict of Nantes, revocation of (1685), 68
Edling, Max, 16, 31, 39, 42
Edwards, Jonathan, 70, 72
Election of 1800, 107, 111, 116–17, 120
Elizabeth I (queen of England), 48, 51
Ellis, Joseph, 13, 27, 113
Era of Good Feelings, 129–30
Erie Canal, 129, 132
evangelicalism, 5, 71–72, 122–23

Father Rale's War (1722–25). *See* Rale, Sebastien
federalism, 4, 31, 39, 102
Federalist Party, 22, 106–7, 110, 116–19, 131–32
Federalist, The, 34, 88. *See also* United States Constitution: ratification debates
Ferguson, Adam, 88
Ferling, John, 5, 109–120
Fischer, David Hackett, 13, 113
Fitzpatrick, Ellen, 15
food, 2, 10, 91–97
Foucault, Michel, 3
founders, 5, 18, 20–22, 27, 31, 101, 108, 114, 118
Founding Brothers. See Ellis, Joseph
framers, 4, 22, 102
France, 20, 26, 111, 117
Franklin, Benjamin, 13, 19, 90, 95 101, 112
Franklin, William, 89
Freeman, Joanne, 10
French and Indian War (1756–63), 110. *See also* Seven Years' War
French North American colonies, 11, 26, 54, 70, 126
Frobisher, Martin, 47

Index

From Resistance to Revolution. See Maier, Pauline
Fundamental Orders (Connecticut), 103

Gales, Joseph, 130
Galloway, Joseph, 111–12, 115
George II (king of Great Britain), 69, 82
George Washington: Man and Monument. See Cunliffe, Marcus, 113
Gipson, Lawrence Henry, 26
Gilbert, Sir Humphrey, 48, 50
Glorious Revolution (1688–89), 67–68, 123–26
Gorton, Samuel, 104
Gray, Edward G., 4, 41–42
Great Awakening (1740s), 67, 69, 83–84,
Great Britain, 11, 26, 30, 68–69, 71–72, 83, 87, 91, 95, 110–11, 115–16, 119, 122–26
Greenblatt, Stephen, 3
Greene, Jack P., 10, 21–22, 24, 25, 31, 33, 42
Gunpowder Plot (1605), 70, 121

Habermas, Jürgen, 3, 29
Hakluyt, Richard, 47–52
Hamilton, Alexander, 13, 88–89, 106–7
Hamiltonianism, 22, 39, 116, 119
Harrington, James, 86
Harrison, William Henry, 96
Hartford Convention (1814–15), 131
Hartwell, Ephriam, 79
Hartwell, William, 76–77
Hartz, Louis, 13, 25
Harvard College, 83–89
Harvard University, 10, 37, 42
Hatherley, Timothy, 66
Hendrickson, David, 31, 39, 42
Henry, Patrick, 96
Higginbotham, Don, 4, 41
historiography: coherence of, 3–4; cultural history, 9, 15, 26, 28, 40, 43, 109, 117; diplomatic history, 36, 43; disjunction between colonial and Revolutionary periods, 4, 9–13, 18–19, 24–26, 28, 31, 41–42; impact of ethnography on, 2; military history, 35–36, 43, 109, 112–13, 120; periodization, 3; political history, 5, 12, 14–16, 27, 29–31, 34–36, 38, 43, 110, 113, 118; reading public's interests, 5, 13, 27–28, 42, 113; whig-gish tendencies, 3, 22, 122, 124; women's history and treatment of gender, 2–3, 9, 12, 15, 25, 39
history education, 14–15
History's Memory. See Fitzpatrick, Ellen
Hoar, John, 78
Hoeveler, J. David, 5. *See also* colonial colleges
Hopkins, Samuel, 87–88
House of Burgesses (Virginia), 102
Hume, David, 35, 88
husbandry, 5, 60, 73–82, 93–94
Hutcheson, Francis, 88
Hutchinson, Anne, 104

Ideological Origins of the American Revolution. See Bailyn, Bernard
imperialism, 19, 38
Indians, 3, 11–12, 20–21, 54–55, 58, 59, 63–64, 70, 74, 93, 102, 105, 116. *See also* Iroquois; Massasoit; Nanepashemet; Pocahontas; Powhatan Indians; Wabanakis
Inheriting the Revolution. See Appleby, Joyce
Invasion of America. See Jennings, Francis
Iroquois, 101–2, 105
Isaacson, Walter, 13, 27, 113

Jackson, Andrew, 130
Jacobites, 69
Jacobs, Margaret, 16
James I (king of England), 52, 121
James II (king of England), 68, 70
Jamestown, 5, 47, 52, 53–58, 102
Jay, John, 88, 111
Jefferson, Thomas, 13, 20–22, 30, 32, 33, 35, 88, 96, 97, 107, 110, 115–19
Jennings, Francis, 63
John Adams. See McCullough, David
Johnson, Samuel, 84
Jones, William, 75
Journal of American History, 10, 14

Kames, Lord (Henry Home), 88
Keayne, Robert, 105

Keegan, John, 120
Kelso, William, 56
Kidd, Thomas S., 5. *See also* Puritans
King, Rufus, 131
King's College (Columbia), 88
Kipling, Rudyard, 19
Kohn, Richard, 112
Kornblith, Gary, 14

Langdon, George D., 65–66
Langdon, Samuel, 89
Laser, Carol, 14
Latin America, 16, 26
Lawson, John, 93
Lee, Richard Henry, 89
Lepore, Jill, 10
liberty, 21, 65, 95; "empire of liberty," 11, 107
Locke, John, 86, 88
London, 49, 56, 65, 104, 111, 124
loyalists, 30, 42, 88–89, 111

Madison, James, 13, 16, 86, 88, 132
Maier, Pauline, 4–5, 18, 24–27, 29–31, 33–34, 37–39
Mancall, Peter C., 5. *See also* Hakluyt, Richard
Mandeville, Sir John, 48–49, 51
Manning, James, 90
Marketplace of Revolution. *See* Breen, T. H.
Marsh, George Perkins, 74
Martyr, Peter (Pietro Martire d'Anghiera), 52
Massachusetts Bay Colony, 54, 59, 66, 75, 83, 103–5
Massasoit (Osamequen), 64
Masur, Louis P., 128–29
Mather, Cotton, 70–71, 84
Mather, Increase, 84–85
Mayflower Compact, 59, 61–63, 104
McConville, Brendan, 1–4
McCullough, David, 13, 27, 113
McWilliams, James E., 5. *See also* food; national identity
Merchant, Carolyn, 74
Meriam, John, 77
Mexico, 26, 48
Middle Colonies, 55, 72, 94
Millar, John, 88

Montaigne, Michel de, 49
Morgan, Edmund S., 13, 24, 27, 33, 38, 56
Morgan, Helen M., 38
Morison, Samuel Eliot, 24, 62, 65–66
Morris, Gouverneur, 88
Morris, Richard B., 24
Murrin, John, 24

Nader, Laura, 101
Nanepashemet (Anthony Pollard), 64
Nash, Gary B., 38
National Endowment for the Humanities, 14–15, 43
national identity, 5, 29–30, 91–99
Nelson, John, 24
Nettles, Curtis, 24
New England, 9, 18, 38, 53–56, 61, 64–65, 67–70, 72, 73–77, 80–81, 83–84, 88, 90, 92, 93, 94, 102–5, 115, 129–32
New England Confederation, 105
Newfoundland, 50, 66
New Haven, 66, 85, 89, 103, 105
New Orleans, battle of (1815), 130
Newport, 87, 89, 95, 104
New York City, 84, 89, 95, 115
Norridgewock, Maine, 70
North, Douglass C., 16
Northwest Passage, 47–48
Norton, Arthur Percival, 65
Norton, Mary Beth, 38
Novak, William, 16

Onuf, Peter S., 4, 21–22, 27, 39, 42
Organization of American Historians, 9

Paine, Thomas, 41, 116–17
Painter, William, 113–14
Parmenius, Stephen, 50
Pasley, Jeffrey, 31
patriots, 30, 42, 86
Peace Pact. *See* Hendrickson, David
Peripheries and Center. *See* Greene, Jack P.
Philadelphia, 83, 89–90, 95, 101, 110, 115
Pilgrims, 5, 53–56, 59–66
Pilgrim Society, 60
Plymouth Colony, 5, 53–54, 56, 59–66, 104–5. *See also* Pilgrims
Pocahontas, 54
Pocock, J. G. A., 21, 33

Index

political culture, 4–5, 29, 40, 86, 90, 122–27
popular history. *See* historiography: reading public's interests
Powhatan Indians, 55
Pownall, Thomas, 21
Presbyterians, 83–85, 89–90
Prince, Thomas, 71
Pufendorf, Samuel, 86
Puritans, 67–72, 83, 87, 103–4, 121
Pursuits of Happiness. See Greene, Jack P.

Quakerism, 65, 85, 94, 121
Quasi-War with France (1798–1800), 111
Quebec, 68
Queen's College (Rutgers), 83, 84, 89
Quinn, David Beers, 51

Radicalism of the American Revolution. See Wood, Gordon S.
Rahe, Paul A., 4, 43
Rakove, Jack N., 4, 14, 27, 42
Rale, Sebastien, 70–71
Ramusio, Giovanni Battista, 50
republicanism, 39, 88, 125
Revolution in Favor of Government. See Edling, Max
Rhode Island, 87, 94, 103–5, 131
Rhode Island College (Brown), 83–84, 90
Roanoke, 51, 57–58
Robertson, Andrew W., 31
Rothenberg, Winifred, 73
Rowe, John, 121
Rowse, A. L., 65
royalism, 122–27
Royster, Charles, 40
Rutman, Darrett B., 65

Salem witchcraft trials (1692), 67
Scituate, Mass., 65–66
Scottish Enlightenment, 88, 90
Second Bank of the U.S., 132
Second Great Awakening, 132
Seven Years' War (1756–63), 124, 126
Shirer, William L., 114
Skeen, C. Edward, 5
Sidney, Algernon, 88
slave trade, 9, 12, 26, 88
slavery, 3, 9–12, 36, 38, 93, 114–16

Smith, Adam, 88
Smith, John, 53–56, 58
Smith, William, 85, 90
Sons of Liberty, 86
Spanish New World empire, 11–12, 26, 47–48
Stamp Act Crisis. See Morgan, Edmund S. and Morgan, Helen, M.
Standish, Miles, 56, 66
Stiles, Ezra, 89

Tariff of 1816, 132
Tart, Thomas, 66
Taylor, Alan, 2–4, 11, 26
Thoreau, Henry David, 74, 80, 109
tobacco, 56–58, 94, 102, 121
Tocqueville, Alexis de, 132
Trachtenberg, Jeffrey, 13

United States, 2, 10, 11, 14, 16, 19, 20, 30, 35, 36, 41, 54–55, 59, 95, 97, 106–8, 110, 119, 132
United States Constitution, 15–18, 21, 27, 28, 30, 33, 37, 39, 40, 41, 101, 114, 128, 130: ratification debates, 16–17, 27, 28, 30, 31, 34
United States Library of Congress, 101

Van Buren, Martin, 96
Vassall, William, 66
Vaughan, Alden T., 65
Virginia, 51–52, 53, 58, 66, 94, 102, 105–6, 121
Virginia Company (of London), 51, 54, 102, 104

Wabanakis Indians, 70
Waldstreicher, David, 10, 31
Walker, Jacob, 78
War of 1812, 130–31
Washington, George, 13, 111–13, 118–19
Washington's Crossing. See Fischer, David Hackett
Webb, John, 71
Wentworth, John, 85, 90
Wheelock, Eleazar, 85, 90
Whig ideology, 42, 88, 90
White, John, 58
Whitefield, George, 71

Willett, Thomas, 66
William and Mary (king and queen of England), 68
William and Mary Quarterly, 14, 31
Williams, Roger, 64, 104
Willison, George F., 60–62, 65
Winlsow, Edward, 60, 63–66
Winthrop, John, 66, 87
Witherspoon, John, 88–89
Wood, Gordon S., 1, 16, 27, 33, 38, 101, 110, 114
Wood, Peter H., 38

Woodmason, Charles, 91
Wright, Edward, 78
Wythe, George, 88

Yale College, 73, 83–89
Yale University, 13, 34, 36
Young, Arthur, 74

Zagarri, Rosemarie, 27
Zelizer, Julian, 16
Zilversmit, Arthur, 12

www.ingramcontent.com/pod-product-compliance
Lightning Source LLC
Chambersburg PA
CBHW031434150426
43191CB00006B/514